Improvement Association West Ewing

The West Ewing Improvement Association

Proceedings of Anniversary Meeting...

Improvement Association West Ewing

The West Ewing Improvement Association
Proceedings of Anniversary Meeting...

ISBN/EAN: 9783337002763

Printed in Europe, USA, Canada, Australia, Japan

Cover: Foto ©Suzi / pixelio.de

More available books at **www.hansebooks.com**

The

West Ewing

Improvement

Association.

Proceedings of Anniversary Meeting, held in Ewing Church, Sept. 2d, 1880, and other valuable matter.

TRENTON, N. J.:
MACCRELLISH & QUIGLEY, STEAM POWER PRINTERS.
1880.

TABLE OF CONTENTS.

OUR MOTTO.

"One for All and All for One."

OUR PRIZES.

I. This Association offers to the resident of Ewing Township who shall set out and maintain the longest and best row of trees along the public highway, in conformity with By-Law II, or the recommendations of Mr. Northrop's address, a PRIZE OF TWENTY-FIVE DOLLARS, payable September 1st, 1881.

II. This Association offers to the Board of School Trustees of either the Scudder's Falls, Birmingham or Brookville District, which shall effect the greatest material improvement in or about the school-house of their district, before July 1st, 1881, a PRIZE OF TWENTY-FIVE DOLLARS, payable on that date, and to be used by the Trustees receiving it for further improvements of an æsthetic nature.

See, also, By-Law I.

THE
West Ewing Improvement Association.

ANNIVERSARY MEETING.

PHONOGRAPHICALLY REPORTED BY GEORGE E. MILES.

The proceedings were opened with prayer by the Rev. S. T. Lowrie, D.D., after which it was moved that the reading of the minutes of the last meeting be dispensed with. The motion was adopted.

The Treasurer, Mr. Charles J. Fisk, then presented his report, which was adopted.

The Committee on Election of Officers then reported, through its chairman, the following names for officers of the Association for the ensuing year:

President—A. B. Green.
Vice-Presidents—Wm. A. Hough, John H. Scudder.
Secretary—John V. Green.
Treasurer—Chas. J. Fisk.

The report was accepted and the officers named were declared elected.

The President, Mr. A. B. Green, in introducing the first speaker, spoke as follows:

It may be well to state that the object of this meeting is to further the cause we are engaged in as an association. The object for which the Association was established two years ago is well known, probably, to all. It is to beautify our homes in the neighborhood, and make this township a more pleasant and desirable place to live in. We have accomplished something in these last two years. Through our direct influence about two hundred shade trees have been set out along the roads and sidewalks. We have made a piece of road which we think is a pattern for the whole county—a road which formerly bore the reputation of being the worst in the place. We have found, in conferring together, that much yet remains to be done, but we are assured that, by co-operation, we can do still more. The setting out of these two hundred trees has been done with great cheerfulness, mostly by people owning the property on which the trees are planted, and as the work proceeds I suppose greater interest will be excited. The road I mentioned a moment ago has cost the township nothing, having been made by voluntary labor and subscription. It is true that prejudices have existed in our community, as I suppose they exist in all. These are a great hindrance to our progress; but we can overcome them by union among ourselves and interchange of views and plans. We are, of course, very tenacious of our own opinions, and think we know a great deal about how this, that and the other thing ought to be done; but, after all, we must admit that our own wisdom cannot be compared to the long experience of those who have carefully studied and scientifically investigated the matter. We find ourselves, by frequent comparison of views, more and more of a like opinion; we establish and improve our social intercourse. One gentleman will be found to know better than another how to plant a tree, or how to trim one; another knows better how to plant or trim a hedge; some lady possesses a rare flower, or knows precisely how to raise one, and through our monthly meetings we gain this varied knowledge and profit by it.

We could name instances where the conditions of health have been improved, but, inasmuch as we have others with us who can instruct us on these important topics, we will listen to them, and we hope, through the dissemination of such ideas, to see more unite with us, until it becomes the interest and business of the entire neighborhood.

I have the honor to introduce to you the Hon. B. G. Northrop, Secretary of the Connecticut State Board of Education.

Address of Hon. B. G. Northrop.

Mr. President, Ladies and Gentlemen—It seems to me very fitting that the gentlemen who served so successfully during the past year should be unanimously re-elected; and if you will only tell us how it is that such nicely-made roads as those you have been completing the past year could be made for four dollars out of the treasury, we would like to carry the art into Connecticut, for it certainly costs *us* a great deal more. I have been delighted—first, in seeing what the plan is, as stated in the village improvement paper, and then in driving about the town this afternoon and observing what has actually been accomplished. I congratulate you on your complete success in driving out of Ewing the "placard" nuisance, or advertising fiend; for I have not seen a single one of those abominations —which in Connecticut are prohibited by law under severe penalties—on any fence, or barn, or board, anywhere in the drive which it has been my privilege to take. I am very glad to see that already you have planted so extensively the fine Osage orange hedge [See Note]—perhaps, for this climate, one of the very best, and one which in future will be a great adornment to the place; and that you are starting so grandly in the planting of trees; and I am pleased, also, with the statement just made that nearly all the trees planted have been set out by the farmers who owned the adjoining land. You are indeed to be congratulated that such a forward step has been taken in the very important matter of roads. [See Note.] The *road* has been, in all ages, the index of the civilization of any country or community. If we had no other remains of the civilization and intelligence of the ancient Roman Empire, its grand, old roads, as they still stand, would tell us the story; for they show the highest of all ancient civilization. If there is progress in any community, the roads will indicate the fact. I have been glad to see, as at Scudder's Falls, so much improvement made around the school-house by the introduction of that neat hedge of American arbor vitæ. It was cheering to notice that on the lawn at the left side as you come out (which the children had been requested not to tread upon), not a foot-fall, or a trace of one, was impressed on that ground reserved for turf.

I noticed, on the way up from New York City, very beautiful adornments around many of the railway stations on the line of the Jersey Central. That is one of the improvements which, I have no doubt, you will incite the railway managers to apply here. You are doing so much for yourselves that it will be a very little thing for you to ask the corporation to appropriate a section of land here and there, at a station which is to become so important in the future, for the purpose of a park. I was delighted the other day, traveling along on the Shore line, to find a beautiful little park at the railway station of Brockton, New York, on the Lake Shore & Michigan Southern Road. I said to the depot agent, "How is this?" He replied, "The superintendent desires us to improve our grounds." "How does he communicate that desire to you?" "Well," said the depot agent, "he sends out a printed circular." I afterward secured one of these circulars, and it read as follows: "The depot master is required to occupy his leisure, and the leisure of the hands, in adorning the grounds, and to see that there is no rubbish or disfigurement anywhere around the railway station." As a result, this depot agent had developed that beautiful little park. I counted there two hundred and forty-six flowers of different kinds, besides some thirty different varieties of trees. It was a gem. Other railways are beginning to do the same thing. North Conway and Plymouth, in New Hampshire; Stonington and Pomfret, in Connecticut; Auburn and Kingston, in Rhode Island, are good illustrations. The Pennsylvania Central is setting a good example all along the line for forty miles west of Philadelphia; and a little persuasion on the part of this Association will carry the point with the railway managers at this depot.

On conference with friends here, I think it better to have an off-hand talk with you, and, therefore, throw aside the written lecture which I had arranged to deliver.

The question has been asked, What has been done in the way of rural improvement elsewhere? and I say "rural," rather than "village" improvement. I discard the word "village," for in towns where I am working, I want to carry out the idea that this business concerns everybody in the township, and we cannot bring about the best results unless we benefit all sections and all classes, and thus secure the co-operation of every citizen. I want every one, however distant, to feel that he has some, however remote, concern in this rural improvement. What is the history of these associations?

1. The first rural improvement association, so far as I know, was formed in New Haven, in 1799, under the lead of James Hillhouse, the leading subscriber and manager. He called it the Village Green Association, and secured a subscription of $1,500. One man, in the generosity of his great heart, subscribed five gallons of rum—as good as gold, according to the theory of that day. You may be sure it was not benzine, as you cannot, what you get now. What has been the result of that grand enterprise? Why, all the majestic elms, nearly, of New Haven were planted then; and it is due to that Association, started at that time, that New Haven is known throughout the land and over the world as the "Elm City," while its beauty, acquired through these magnificent trees, has attracted great numbers of wealthy citizens, so that the annual taxes on the property there attracted by the existence of the great elms exceed by far all that the elms ever cost.

As far as I can learn, the next volunteer association was founded about fifty years ago, in Heidelberg. Suffice it to say, the efforts of that association in rebuilding the old castle, and repairing the magnificent drive-way up to it, is the secret, together with the planting their beautiful avenues and parks with fine trees, of the fact that you find, on an average, eight hundred English residents there, to say nothing of the hundreds that flock there from other sources. To name two or three other European illustrations—many of you have seen how attractive Baden-Baden and Wiesbaden, in Germany, and Interlaken, in Switzerland, have been made by similar rural adornments. The Swiss understand making their homes attractive. Out of 485,000 households, about 465,000 in Switzerland are householders. You cannot match that in America; and there are no people on the face of this globe, unless it be the Japanese, who love their country more, and are more devoted to its interests, than are the Swiss.

More than a century ago, a grand work was accomplished (though not by a rural improvement association) in a town in Connecticut, which was a subject of conversation at the dinner-table to-day, and thus was brought to my mind. It was the town of Stratford. Dr. Samuel Johnson, once rector at Stratford and afterwards president of Kings College (since the Revolution, Columbia College), New York City, visiting England and the estate of Alexander Pope, at Twickenham, was struck with the beauty of the Syrian willow growing there. The tradition is, that about a hundred and fifty years ago, an English merchant doing business in Aleppo and Smyrna, brought the poet a package of figs incased in a basket of unpeeled osiers. Noticing that one of the scions penetrating into the moist figs was budding, Pope carefully planted it. Thence grew the famous Twickenham willow that became a favorite with the poet, and finally with the English people. President Johnson brought scions to Stratford, whence it was widely spread through New England and New York. This incident intensified the interest of the Johnson family in tree planting, who took the lead in this grand work in Stratford. No town of its size on the Shore Line, between New York and Boston, is adorned with so many stately, ancient trees as this. Much as this willow was admired for private grounds, with its long, drooping pendants, it was not deemed best for public streets, for which the elm, maple, plane, and other natives were wisely preferred. Now there is nothing but its broad avenues adorned with noble trees, especially to distinguish Stratford from any other of a dozen places along the Shore Line; but, notwithstanding the nuisance of mosquitoes (bred in the adjoining salt marshes), Stratford has attracted many wealthy men, through the exceeding beauty of its streets and avenues. No one goes there without offering up a sentiment of thanksgiving to old Dr. Johnson for the controlling influence he exerted in the beautifying of the town.

But of more recent improvement associations, Stockbridge, Massachusetts, was the pioneer, and that one was started by Mary Hopkins, the niece of President Mark Hopkins, of Williams College. There was no general law of incorporation at that time, but a special act was passed, and that has been in operation some twenty-eight years, and what has been the result? When the association began its work, Stockbridge was a wild, rugged place. I remember it when, in my boyhood, I traveled through the Housatonic valley. Now it is, by far, the most beautiful town in all New England. When Miss Hopkins, now

Mrs. J. C. Goodrich, inaugurated this association, (and it may be a good hint to continue this plan of having an annual festival,) the idea was adopted of having, on the fourth Wednesday in August, a gathering of the people from all parts of the town, on a common platform, without reference to party or denomination, and that idea has been carried out and kept up to this day. They claim that nature has always smiled upon them, as she does upon you this afternoon, and that they have sunny heavens above them on anniversary day. They have had poems, addresses and post-prandial speeches, and the re-unions have done them good, and stirred them to new enterprise and energy.

One of the grandest results of these associations, as it should ever be, is the promotion of fraternal feeling. In many country towns there is needless strife. Such alienations destroy the charm of country homes. Everything should be done to bind the people together in the ties of a common interest, and you can do that in no way so well as by bringing them to work together, as you are working for yourselves. The beautiful decorations of this church to-day are profuse beyond what I have ever seen. I perceive in each of the slips two or three bouquets, besides the ferns and other flowers, and these fitting symbols of the sheaf of wheat. I say this does you good. It has benefited the ladies whose labors have accomplished this result. The interests, the sympathies, the friendly feelings of this whole community, have been drawn out, and they will be more likely to co-operate in the good work for improvement; and I feel sure that this sacred place, instead of being desecrated, is hallowed by its occupation at this time, for a purpose so entirely in unison with all the sacred designs of the church.

I happened to be called upon to give the anniversary address at the quarter-centennial at Stockbridge, and as the Treasurer read his report, after giving certain details he said: "Every acre of land and every homestead in Stockbridge has appreciated by reason of the work of this association." As many of you know, wealthy men have been attracted thither from far and near. Meeting a wealthy New York merchant, known to many of you, up there, one day, I said: "What brought you here?" "Well," said he, "I happened to be passing through Stockbridge, one Summer, and I noticed how neat the streets were, and how the grounds and surroundings of the houses were adorned, and I thought a home here would have increased attractions and a higher value." And so he put up his elegant mansion there, and the same has been done by many others, and Stockbridge is full of the homes of wealthy people.

What has their improvement association done there? They first looked out for the planting of trees, and after all the streets were amply supplied, they turned their attention to the side-walks. Every one agreed there to look out for his own frontage. I remember driving around the place on one occasion, with the lady who founded the association, and if anywhere, three, four, five or six miles away from the center, she found weeds growing in the road-way, she jogged the memory of the farmer, and the road was cleaned by those who owned the adjoining property. That will be the result in Ewing. I noticed, in driving along to-day, that in a number of roads where you have put out lines of trees, there are some ugly weeds growing alongside the fence, It will be a very easy matter to have those cut down once or twice or thrice a season, and it will add greatly to the beauty of the place. They look out for that at Stockbridge, and, as one thing led to another, there soon came along a former son of Stockbridge, and, seeing what had been done, he said: "I must have a hand in this," and so he gave them $20,000 for a library. Another man said, "I will join in this good work, and give them a library building." So they have there a beautiful library and reading-room, and keep it in operation. It all springs from the interest awakened among the whole people, by a village improvement association. I have no time for further details regarding the work of this enterprising organization. I have talked at their anniversaries many times. I have found them all aglow with enthusiasm.

Ten years ago, visiting New Milford, Connecticut, I met there two young ladies, to whom I said: "You ought to start a rural improvement association here." They decided to do so, and set to work. I gave them the plans. They got up a fair that netted $800, and what has been the result? From a rough, rugged town, New Milford has been made the most beautiful town in the State of Connecticut. No town in the country, in the same limits of time, has made such a complete transformation. There was a wide street, but the carts, crossing in all directions, had cut the road up. In wet weather a brook ran through the center; in dry times there was an unseemly line of mud. They ran a sewer through the whole, leveled the ground, enclosed it, made concrete sidewalks, and a little ribbon of lawn between the fences and the sidewalk and between the sidewalk and gutter. Then came the drive-way on each side, and a parallelogram was formed, and adorned with flowers and trees. I was in New Milford the other day, and a prominent gentleman said: "Well, we spend money pretty freely, but nobody grumbles." It has not been done from taxation at all; all is voluntary; but no one would go back to the barbaric condition that existed ten years ago, even were it necessary to spend ten-fold more. As at Stockbridge, they are appreciating the results in the rise of real estate and the increased demand for homes and lands in the town.

Many of you know of the present beauty of Litchfield. Perhaps some of you saw an article in the New York papers some time ago, about the beauty of Litchfield. The place was living on the laurels of the last century, and was going into decay, and everything was neglected; but seven years ago they started an association of this kind. I met, while there, a wealthy gentleman from one of our cities. "What led you to come up here," said I. "Well," said he, "you would not have got me to come up here if the old fogy spirit prevailed as it did ten years ago; but I found there was a new life and interest here, and it was worth while to have a Summer home here." And he erected his stately mansion there, and luxuriates in his delightful home every Summer. Their boarding-houses and hotels are not ample enough to accommodate the parties that desire to go there. Not having the advantage of such sanitary wisdom as Col. Waring would have given them, the place was desolated, needlessly, by a terrible fever, a few years ago, simply through the neglect of drainage. It was the place of all others that ought to be the healthiest; but those very country towns, where there is every opportunity of securing the purest water and best air, sometimes are needlessly ravaged by diphtheria and typhoid fever and other kindred troubles, which proper care and foresight would prevent.

I have in mind a little town in Connecticut—Middlebury—with less than eight hundred population, and very scanty means. I suppose that whole township has not one-tenth of the valuation of Ewing; and yet, by getting everybody enlisted in the cause, and thus, by co-operation, they have improved the village green, and the farmers have taken hold of the matter, and said, "We will have no rubbish, no weeds, nothing to disfigure our homesteads." You will sometimes go to a village and find everything neat, in the main, and yet the homes of some neglectful men will be disfigured by broken cart-wheels, or piles of lumber or chips, or decaying rubbish of one sort or another. Everything of that kind is cleared away from that little village, and, with only a few farmers along the road, they have agreed to keep it in good condition. I might give many other details, but have not time for that.

The question asked me since coming here is, how to raise the funds? Probably you know better how to answer that question than I can tell you, because you have among you liberal men who have already contributed generously to these grand results, and because the detailed plans must always be determined by local conditions; but I say, in general—

1. Enlist the ladies. Many of our most successful associations have been started by ladies, and all need their sympathy and efficient co-operation. I always feel sure of success in any town where two or three earnest ladies take hold of this matter. This is woman's special sphere.

2. Interest the youth of the town in this good work. Give the children something to do in improving the grounds and surroundings of their homes, if not the road-sides. The New York "Evening Post" well says: "They, more readily than anybody else, become interested in such matters, and they may easily be induced to bring trees from the forest, and to plant them where they are needed, without cost to anybody, and without other than willing and eager work. How great the good is that boys and girls derive from *their own active interest* in such things, every attentive observer of youth knows. *The educational effect* of such employments and interests, the refining influence, the æsthetic improvement wrought, the enlargement of heart and mind which grow, directly and indirectly, out of

work of this kind, done by *united* effort by the boys and girls of a town, under the stimulus of public approval, are not to be set down in words or expressed in figures. In any town, where juvenile enthusiasm is awakened in public improvement, the schools will accomplish better results, the library will be more freely and profitably used, there will be less idleness, less wrong-doing, habits will be better, aspirations higher, the tone of life stronger. Every such town must improve in intelligence, taste, public spirit and morality, which is decency of life reduced to principle, quite as positively as it grows in external beauty.

3. Get subscriptions from the more willing or wealthy residents.

4. Invite the co-operation of non-resident sons of the town, whom fortune has favored, who are often glad to gratefully remember the mother soil that bore them, and thus build a monument, each for himself, and be henceforth gratefully recognized as the benefactor of his townsmen and of future generations. A beautiful village of tasteful, happy homes, would be a proud monument for any man. There is a rare luxury in witnessing the fruits of one's benefactions, *giving while living* and able to enjoy the rich results, rather than leaving legacies to be lessened or lost in the wrangles of contending heirs.

5. Money may be raised by the annual payment of membership fees, or by life memberships.

6. In some towns, fairs are held to raise money for this purpose.

7. In some instances, prizes have been offered for tree planting —giving, for example, $75, $50, $40 and $30 for the longest and best rows of trees by any road-side. Two hundred dollars, offered in this way, in one town, stimulated an extraordinary interest in tree planting.

As I have intimated, one of the prime ends which we keep in view in the fifty or sixty associations which we have in Connecticut, is to cultivate public spirit, and foster town pride. These are sentiments of great influence and great value, and the want of them is greatly to be deplored, for it indicates a serious defect of character. The man who does not love to honor and cherish the town that gave him birth, has no heart in his bosom. I have in mind a railway king, a millionaire, who never visits the town where he first saw the light, but leaves his old homestead to decay, and neglect, and slight; and his character corresponds with his actions. The cold, selfish, sinister soul is sterile in heroic virtues, but the sentiment which honors one's homestead and one's town, is noble and ennobling. It is a prime element of true manhood, and has ever characterized the greatest and best of men.

I need not say a word on the prospective influence of this association in promoting public health, when you have secured the services of a gentleman so thoroughly competent to discuss this subject. Some of our country towns, naturally favorable to health and longevity, have suffered fearfully and needlessly from the ravages of diseases, evidently caused by neglect of hygienic laws. In many towns, great improvement has been made in the matter of drainage, removal of waste, and guarding wells and water supplies from impurities.

Your association, starting so vigorously, will, I am confident, accomplish grand results in improving the roads and road-sides and planting trees, not only within your own limits, but in creating a healthy public sentiment which will extend the good work through all the approaches to the town. I would like to have you give an invitation to Trenton to meet you at your boundary line with a continuous line of trees on every road that runs towards Trenton; and I believe that, under the influence of my esteemed friend, the friend and superintendent of the public schools, Hon. E. A. Apgar, Trenton would accept the challenge. There are many pretty towns that give such challenges, one to another, and carry them out, too. It is easy enough to accomplish, if you can succeed once in arousing ambition.

Many of the roads in England and France are made enchanting by these continuous lines of trees. You remember the story of the two men who laid a wager that each could tell the prettiest region in England, and they chose an umpire, and paid him the money. Then each wrote his decision, and, on handing them over to the umpire, it was found that the choice of one was the road from Kenilworth to Coventry, and the other's selection was the road from Coventry to Kenilworth; and the main attraction of this road was the magnificent trees that shaded the route. Among those trees, some of you will remember that grand old tree, the Cedar of Lebanon. It is not of very rapid growth, but it is worth trying, and your children and children's children will thank you for it. I have no doubt it may be grown here. It thrives in Philadelphia. My friend at my right was educated at East Hartford, and he remembers the grand old avenues of elms there. I can hardly tell you how magnificent those triple rows of trees are. When the French forces under Rochambeau were stationed at East Hartford, for their Winter quarters, Rochambeau, according to the traditions of that day, said: "Now, boys, let's give them a specimen of French taste." Just at that time [illegible] had been in the habit of planting trees on the way-sides in France for hundreds of miles. So the boys set to work and planted those magnificent elms, which occur at short intervals from Windsor down through East Hartford to Glastenbury. Grander ones it would be hard to find. Thanks to Rochambeau.

One of the aims of village improvement should be the making of sidewalks. There is room for much to be done in that direction here. Perhaps the gravel is not at hand. The ordinary coal ashes spread along, the coarser below and the finer on top, make a very good substitute, and it can very easily and cheaply be accomplished. [See Note.]

To quicken the intellectual life of the people, is one aim of these associations. The founding of libraries is an important aid in this direction. The supply of good books increases the demand. A taste for books has been awakened in many towns by a well-selected library, where the improvement has been as marked in the quality as in the quantity of the books read. Such a library naturally becomes the pride and treasure of a town, rendering it a more desirable place of residence and adding attractions to every intelligent home within its limits.

The formation of book clubs favors the intellectual improvement of a community. A score or more associate together and agree each to pay from one to five dollars a year for the purchase of a sort of circulating library. Sometimes they meet once a month to discuss and vote upon the books to be purchased, thus promoting social improvement as well as mental culture. The books are circulated among the members in rotation, the members retaining volumes each a fortnight. At the end of the year, these books are sold at a low rate, and often to the members, and the avails used for the purchase of other books. The books usually selected are travels, histories, biographies, popular treatises on science and philosophy, and sometimes books of choice poetry and romance. Good fellowship, as well as intellectual improvement, are sometimes promoted by organizing *reading* circles. Selections in prose and poetry, often a play of Shakespeare, the several parts having been previously assigned, are the subjects of careful study and drill. The social influence of these weekly circles is sometimes extended by a rehea[illegible] more public character. The support of a village reading-room, supplied with the leading journals of the day —daily, weekly, monthly or bi-monthly—is a good result accomplished in many towns. A course of lyceum lectures is sustained by many rural improvement associations, the profits of which is their "benefit," while the social opportunities thus opened are clear gain.

An annual festival under the direction of the rural improvement association, tends to deepen public interest in this work, and to fraternize the whole people of a town. In some towns, literary exercises, addresses and music fill the programme, and occasionally, though not commonly, a collation and post-prandial speeches become another bond of union and fellowship. In the rigid, and sometimes frigid, state of rural life too often found among us, we need more heartily to cultivate the social amenities and learn the art of "turning work into play." The supposed monotony and dullness of country life drive many to the city. It is wise for our farmers to multiply occasions for social enjoyment. The arbor-day festival may help to counteract the tendency of rural life to isolation and seclusion, lifting out of the ruts of a plodding monotony, promoting neighborly feeling and strengthening social ties. The rural laborers in Switzerland and Germany socialize far more than American farmers. Their festive spirit is a strongly-marked feature of their character. It is manifested in the family, in neighborhood greetings and meetings, in schools, in rifle feasts, in processions, and various social gatherings. They have a passion for nature, and love to frequent their beautiful groves and gardens. This genial spirit is everywhere fostered by music, both vocal and instrumental. As a result, there is an inexpressible something in the German character that carries mirthful and happy childhood into old age, giving an added charm to social life, and lightness and cheer to sober work.

Among the minor aims of these associations is the providing of rustic seats under the shades for the comfort of pedestrians. In the beautiful drive in West Ewing along the Delaware, how pleasantly would such simple seats suggest neighborly kindness and courtesy. Also, setting up watering-troughs for horses, at convenient points, where, from adjacent hill-sides, never-failing springs facilitate this improvement; furnishing plans for rural architecture, and for gates and fences; in securing hedge-rows in room of fences; or, better still, *in villages*, combining to remove all fences, so that the private grounds seem to unite with the wayside in one large lawn; the suggestion of neutral tints for dwellings and out-houses, in place of the glaring white formerly so common; arrest of stray cattle, for strolling cattle usually are, and always ought to be, outlawed; preventing nuisances—one of these is the tearing up the turf fronting a dwelling-house, by inconsiderate road menders. Painting or posting advertisements on the rocks or fences by the myriad nostrum makers is a nuisance in my State prohibited by law,* and it should be everywhere forbidden. The same may be said of the encroachments made upon the highway every time the stone wall or fence boundary is rebuilt. The whole township should show an interest in preventing such curtailment of its roadways. A rural improvement association can develop a public sentiment which will of itself correct these evils without occasioning any neighborhood strifes or alienations. In this matter, the interest of one is the interest of all. The motto of the Swiss Confederacy, "One for all, and all for one," is the true motto for the several districts, and for all the people of a township.

Reading associations increase the influence of an organization of this kind very widely, and lectures as well. Its educational bearing is of the very highest consequence. The *taste* should early be cultivated. It should be held to be a religious duty to love the beautiful in nature, the beautiful in art, still more the

---

*Read carefully the law of the State of New Jersey on this matter.—Ed.

beautiful in character; for all the beauties, utilities and grandeurs of nature culminate in the formation of character. In the very structure of our being, God rebukes the ignorance or indolence that so often dwarfs that noble faculty—the love of the beautiful—designed to be an ally of virtue and religion. Your association here will develop in the minds of your children a love of flowers, vines, shrubs and trees, all the stronger because they have helped in planting and cultivating them. In regard to the superior educational influences of rural scenes and scenery and occupations, Dr. Bushnell was wont to say: "In all my reading of history, I do not recollect the name of a truly great man who spent his early life in a great city." Some one said to me the other day, "What about Franklin?" To which I replied: "Franklin grew up in a small village called Boston." It was but a village at that time; and was not incorporated as a city till one hundred and eighteen years after Franklin was born; but would he have been equal to the achievements which the world has admired, if he had been reared in a great city like Paris? Would Washington have been prepared to become the "Father of his Country" if he had been dandled in the lap of affluence in a great city like London?

Nature is the great educator; birds, flowers, insects and all animals are our practical primary teachers. Facts and objects as best seen in the country are the earliest instruments for developing the juvenile faculties. In all our history, the country has proved the great school of mind. Here dwell, and for wise reasons here God intended should dwell, the great majority of mankind.

The country sends far more than its proportion of gifted men to the great centers of influence. It is thus continually enriching the cities, for towards them are flowing, like their streams, the material and mental treasures which have their origin in the mountain springs, and without which the cities would die out. A writer in one of our popular monthlies disparages farmers and farming, saying: "I can pick out the farmer and farmer's boys in any assemblage by their manifest boorishness of looks and action. Your farmer's boy is awkward and jagged, like the oak growing in the open lot, while your city youth is trim and graceful like the pine in the forest." After reading that article, I took a trip to Cape Cod, where a fearful storm had just swept the coast and where were to be seen many a pine made the sport of the tempest, but never an oak stirred from its moorings. So your farmer's boy, trained to industry, to economy of time as well as money, will breast a thousand storms, any one of which would upset your tenderly-reared city youth. "It is not in the great cities, nor in the confined shops of trade, but principally in agriculture, that the best stock or staple of men is grown. It is in the open air—in communion with the sky, the earth and all living things—that the largest inspiration is drunk in and the vital energies of a real man constructed." I often advise the wealthy in our cities to secure Summer homes in the country, or to send their children, for at least one entire year, to the country, with its freer sports and wider range for rambles, and, better still, to give one season to hard work on the farm or in the shop. The practical skill thus gained in adapting means to ends, in observing common objects and animals, may compensate for some loss of book learning, and lead one afterward to pursue text-books with greater zest.

It is the interest of the farmers, of all people on the globe, to co-operate in the work of rural improvement. In no other way can you farmers so surely counteract this excessive mania for the attractions and distractions of city life. We need to enforce in the school, as well as in the family, the necessity and dignity of labor, and its vital connection with all human growth and progress and welfare. The theory that labor is menial, that the tools of the farm or a trade are badges of servility, ought to be refuted in our schools. The Hebrews, acting under divine inspiration, trained up their youth to thoroughly learn some handicraft. When proclaiming the gospel for all the world, Paul could, if need be, earn his livelihood by his trade; and his associates did not dream that they were demeaning themselves or their sacred office by resuming their old business of fishing. Why was it that the Great Teacher, whose life was designed to be the perfect standard of duty to all men in all ages, sought out—yes, *sought out*—the humble cottage of the carpenter, and toiled at the carpenter's bench, except that He might reprobate before the eyes of the world this heathenish notion that labor is servile? It will do for the Chinese mandarin, who lets his nails grow longer than his fingers, to prove that he does not work because he cannot. I say more should be done to dignify farm work; and how can the farmer do this better than by interesting his boys and girls in the adornment of the home and the village?

While I feel a grateful pride in the fact that something in the line of rural adornment has lately been accomplished in all the towns of Connecticut, especially around the homes and grounds of our citizens, I do not mean to slacken my efforts till an efficient association is formed in every township. Though this is no part of my prescribed duties, but only a volunteer avocation in addition to my proper vocation, my interest in the work grows with years and results. It is my ambition to do my utmost to improve the homes and home life of our people, and help them to realize that the highest privilege and central duty of life is the creation of happy homes. The multiplied ministries of nature, providence and religion, center in the maintenance of happy homes. The higher aim of the industries of life, whether agricultural, manufacturing or commercial, and the great end for which government itself is worthy to be sustained, is, that men may live in happy homes. "The hope of America is the homes of America." You improve the schools by improving the homes, as truly as you improve the homes by improving the schools.

It was a very fit thing that, in opening this meeting, we should unite in a prayer of thanksgiving to God for our happy homes, and a fit thing to pray, as we did most fervently and heartily, that we might co-operate in the embellishment of our homes; and let me commend to you, my friends, the spirit of that very appropriate prayer. The hope of Ewing is the homes of Ewing, and when every citizen is induced to look out for his own frontage, and his own grounds, this result is, in the highest degree, secured.

It is a grand fact that modern civilization relates to the homes of the people, especially to their health, thrift, comfort, and their intellectual and moral advancement. In former times, and other lands, men were counted only in the aggregate, and valued only as they helped to swell the revenues and retinues of kings and nobles. The government was the unit, and each individual only added one to the roll of serfs or soldiers, but with us the individual is the unit, and the government is of the people, for the people, and by the people. Every influence should, therefore, be employed with us to foster home attachments. On Cape Cod, the other day, I met a widow, who said to me: "I have not heard from my boy for twelve months, but I know he hain't spoke ship," and she pointed to the flowers and shrubs that her boy had helped to plant; and I knew he had not spoken a ship, for a boy of that kind would not let an opportunity pass, wherever he might be, to cheer her with tidings of his safety. Said a man thirty-five years president of a New England college: "I never knew a boy go far astray who devotedly cherished his mother and truly reverenced his father."

Now, fathers and mothers, if you want to improve your boys, and make them reverence you, keep your homesteads clean, and teach the children to cultivate a love for flowers. I think we have an instance in point in that wonderful people, the Japanese. There are no people on the earth who love flowers as they do; no people who cultivate them so universally. Every one must have flowers in his front yard—*must*, not by imperial edict, but by what is better, universal public sentiment. If, possibly, the local conditions in a narrow street do not permit a plat of flowers, they will then have potted flowers, and the arrangements in the rear for flowers are ample. Was it not a striking fact, at the Centennial Exhibition, that the only foreign bazaar adorned with native flowers and shrubs was the Japanese? and, however the commissioners mourned that they had suffered greatly by the long passage, they were exquisitely beautiful, as you well remember. My home has been fragrant, much of the time the last few years, with bouquets sent by Japanese students, which is their way of expressing gratitude for some little favor given. Then, again, the love of flowers is largely, in my mind, the secret of the wonderful politeness of the Japanese. No people on the face of this globe, in the family or in the school, so thoroughly teach the ethics and æsthetics of etiquette as do the Japanese. The French are also one of the politest peoples in the world, and the love of flowers is one of their characteristics.

I have been requested to say a word as to what trees to plant. Your printed programme specifies a list of trees. I would like to add one or two, while admitting the excellence of those named. I would add the linden, a magnificent tree and very hardy, and the common hemlock. Another noble tree which you have sought to grow is the tulip, and you have failed because you planted it too large. It has a deep root, and should be taken from the nursery young. It is a great mistake to think you are going to gain by planting big trees. If you plant them large, you must crop them, and a tree never recovers thoroughly from the beheading process. There will grow up, perhaps, two limbs and spread out, and then, in a tempest, the tree splits, and never develops its full beauty. I want to urge, also, as a very beautiful tree, which you will find growing across the river in Pennsylvania, at various points, the hickory and the black walnut. They both need to be planted young, and with care, the hickory especially. Let me drop a word of caution—not to plant big trees in little yards. While I advocate tree planting most thoroughly, I want to reiterate the old motto: "*Where the sunlight cannot come, the doctor must.*" Don't let the old Norway spruce stand so near as to shut out all sunlight. Your list of trees, recommended for the roadside, justly includes the elm, which unites the two elements of grace and grandeur more than any other tree. Michaux calls it "the most magnificent vegetable of the temperate zone." No doubt its roots extend further into the adjoining fields than those of any other tree. On this account the hickory, white ash, Norway maple, mountain ash, and especially the tulip, with its straight stem, that may be trimmed high, if need be, should be favorites with the farmers for the road-side. The tulip is a rapid grower, and attains large size, and is unsurpassed in the beauty of its form and foliage.

Of all exotics, I recommend the European larch. You can get it from Douglas & Sons, at Waukegan, Illinois, for $8 or $9 a thousand. It is very hardy, has a perfect root, and probably 990 out of every 1,000 will live. They come in perfect condition. The tree unites three characteristics—rapidity of growth, symmetry of form, and durability of the timber. We are planting it, in Massachusetts and Connecticut, for economical purposes, as well as for adornment. I find there is no need here of reclaiming barren lands, as in a town so fertile you have no sand banks. Further South, I should have dropped a hint about reclaiming sand barrens by planting the trees appropriate for that purpose. The larch is the great timber tree, as well as ornamental tree, at the present time in Europe.

But I notice that I have overrun my time, and, therefore, I stop abruptly; for I would not deprive you of the privilege and pleasure you have of learning the results of the sanitary survey of this place, made by so competent a gentleman as Col. Waring. May I congratulate you on your good fortune in securing such a survey. If any one has doubted the wisdom of it hitherto, I think ten years hence he will be thankful to this Association for this step. I have been surprised again and again, in going into our country towns, to find in the homes of men who thought they had everything in perfection, that the sanitary conditions were imperfect and bad; that the waste-pipe from the kitchen sink, for instance, emptied into a cesspool within six or eight feet of the well, and from it conduits formed in the course of years, so that the water was contaminated; and the most frightful diseases have, within my knowledge, come from drinking water rendered impure by the sink cesspools, which people think little of as injuring the health of the home. But I stop abruptly.

The President then introduced Col. George E. Waring, Jr., of Newport, R. I.

Address of Col. George E. Waring.

Mr. President, Ladies and Gentlemen:—I find myself laboring under a very unaccustomed embarrassment in appearing before you to-day. It is my misfortune to have been compelled to practice the gloomy profession of a Sanitary Engineer. I am seldom called to perform any service except where my labors are sorely needed. If I am sent for to visit a house, it is more than likely that the undertaker has been there before me. When I received the letter of your enthusiastic Mr. Fisk, inviting me to make a sanitary survey of West Ewing, my first thought was: "One more unfortunate!" I fully anticipated, judging from my previous experiences, finding matters so very serious here, and, perhaps, life grown so uncertain, that something would have to be done immediately, at least to maintain the price of your lands. I accordingly sent my assistant here to ferret out the sources of evil in all your houses, and I came yesterday myself to drive through your pestilential marshes, and to investigate your filthy drains. I find, quite to my surprise, that you have sent for the wrong man. It is no such place. In more than one respect this is fortunate, because the hour is getting late, and I shall say very little, for the reason that I have very little to say.

I have no doubt that in what Mr. Northrop has said, and in some things that I may say, there may be the suggestion of an inquiry concerning sanitary matters, which may lead you to desire further information on that subject. If so, I shall be glad to answer any inquiries you may make, and to enlighten you, if I can, on certain points. I beg you to disregard one requirement of the programme, which is that you shall put your questions in writing. I think it altogether unfair that you should be restricted in your method of inquiry, while I shall enjoy the more rapid one of answering your questions directly.

I say, frankly, after looking over so much of your town as is embraced in the province of your Association, that I have found only one serious source of trouble. A more beautiful and generally healthy looking section of country than this which surrounds your church here, I have rarely seen. There are certain bays at the side of the canal and some of the ditches running north and south between the canal and the river, that might be improved, although none of them are so serious as to require much professional advice. The saw-mill pond, on the other hand, is in every respect as bad as it could be. It would take too long for me to enter into a discussion regarding the causes of malaria, and what it is, at least according to our imperfect theories; but any one who has investigated the condition of malarious regions must see that there are, toward the upper end of that pond, conditions of soil such as may be surely depended upon to produce malaria, if they occur in a country where malaria exists at all. From what I see of the sources of supply of that pond, it is evident that when the mill is used the water must be drawn down very rapidly, and a considerable area of wet bank must be left exposed to the sun and air before the water again rises to its level. This is one of the most serious features of the problem. I state the case thus distinctly, because, fortunately, a short time before I came here, Dr. Lowrie took the pains to investigate the condition of the whole population within the immediate neighborhood of that pond. If I remember his figures correctly, he examined into the condition of the occupants of twenty-three houses, and found only two of those houses free from cases of chills and fever. While he does not know the total of population, he says he found fifty-eight cases of chills and fever. From the examination that my assistant has made of the rest of the territory, I should say there were, altogether, not ten cases in the whole remainder of the district. Now the correction of this difficulty is very simple, if means are provided for it; but it is absolutely essential, before that land can be drained and made wholesome, so that the poor people who live in the neighborhood may escape their chills and fever, that the dam should be taken down, the mill-right extinguished, and that land made as sound, in a sanitary sense, as that lying above or below it. I am informed that there are legal steps which may be taken, by virtue of recent action of the Legislature, by the Town Committee as a Board of Health, to remedy defects of this description; but that is, of course, the last resort among neighbors, who have associated themselves together, as you have, in friendly union; and it happens to be a case, if one can judge by the appearance of manufacturing establishments, where the entire value of the mill-right to its owner might be contributed by the members of the Association, or the inhabitants of the town, and thus the problem solved by other than extreme legal measures.

This, as I have said, is the only thing I have seen in the whole district covered by this Association, that is worthy of serious comment. We have examined between forty and fifty houses, and have found in no one of them gross defects such as we too often find in cities, and which are so marked in their unhealthy influence, and so much written about in the newspapers. But it is to be remembered that, if the defects of the country are not so gross as those of the city, they are sometimes more subtle. The sanitary rule has never been better formulated than it was by Hippocrates when he prescribed "Pure Air, Pure Water, and a Pure Soil." I think, if you look about your houses, even here, you will find that you do not, in all cases, live quite up to the requirements of this prescription. We have, all of us, more or less, inherited certain habits of life from our ancestors, who, if they lived healthily, did so rather through good luck than by good management, and who developed some habits which it would be well for their descendants to forget. They had also some advantages which the weather-strip man, and the carpenter, and the stove-maker have taken away from us. In the old houses, however impure the water and soil may have been, there was abundant opportunity, with the help of the open fire-places and the broad cracks, to obtain fresh air.

I find that in every house here, but no more than elsewhere, there is a disregard of the more simple requirements concerning pure air, pure water, and pure soil. For example, your householders are very largely chargeable with ignorance of, or indifferance to, the maxim that Mr. Northrop aptly quoted, "Where the sunlight cannot come, the doctor must." Your trees seem to me to be too large, too near to the houses, and too close together, and I sometimes wondered, as I was passing along, whether there does not run in your veins a strong infusion of the old New York Dutch blood, which leads to the closing of all your front shutters from Saturday until Saturday. *At all events, if the population are still in their own homes, they are certainly living with less direct, pure sunlight than they need and might have by a proper opening of their windows and shutters.*

The cellars of your houses we have found to be generally in good condition, but, from their construction, and from the character of their windows and the uses to which they are put, the idea seems to suggest itself that they are not in such good condition in Winter time. Your cellars are used, to a considerable extent, for storing vegetables, and I imagine that in the Winter time they are a good deal like farm-houses in other States, tightly closed, pretty musty, not always absolutely dry, and generally separated from the living rooms by only the board floor, with no plastering or ceiling underneath.

One habit prevails here, more, I will say, than in New England, and that is the making use of the back yard as a kitchen sink.

Now, if this is done consistently, and faithfully, and intelligently, it is a very good thing. If the house-maid will take pains, each time, to flirt her water on a new place, so as to let the old place dry, under the action of the sun and air, it is certainly as wholesome (though not as tidy) a way of getting rid of kitchen water as can be devised; but this care is very seldom taken, and in many places we have noticed that the water is cast on the same place, and that the land is foul, often very foul, and leading to the greater or less tainting of the well, according to its nearness. *I should say, that in so far as your circumstances are suspicious, you have decidedly to look to your wells. We have seen a good many that are more than suspicious. I would venture to say, without having made a chemical analysis of the water, or a microscopical examination of its contents, that it must, in many cases, be impure, unsafe, and only to be used with risk.* There is one house, for example, in this town, where the well is in the cellar, and where, outside of it, only thirty feet away, there is a vault, eight feet deep, full pretty nearly to the top, and located in soil which I believe would transmit impurities for a considerably greater distance than thirty feet. That is the most extreme case that we have found, although we have seen a good many others where the distance is far within the danger line. Now, it is quite true that you and your ancestors have lived (those who have lived) under these conditions, and have, nevertheless, had a lower death rate than many other places, not so favorably situated as regards soil and exposure.—

At this point the speaker was interrupted by the following question from one of his audience:

Q. Please define what passes beyond the danger line between the vault and the well?

To which the speaker replied:

That depends entirely upon the means of communication between them—whether the soil is composed of clay, of gravel, or of rock, with seams running from one to the other. It can only be determined by using some test, such, for instance, as to put salt water in the vault and to examine for salt in the well; but I should say that there certainly ought to be an interval of more than a hundred feet in such soil as this. It is natural for you to think that the idea that there is danger in such a case is all nonsense, and mere theory and "book-farming," for you have drunk water out of that well, and you know there isn't a better well in the State of New Jersey; your grandfather said there wasn't a better well anywhere round about. Now, such wells—wells held in just as high estimation—have, unfortunately, done great mischief in the world. One of the greatest outbreaks of cholera in London was traced entirely to the impurity of a public well. The *degree* of danger is very well illustrated by a remark made by Mr. Clark, Engineer of the Improve Sewerage of Boston, who said: "The risk is very slight, but it is a risk of a terrible danger." I have recently been reading the report of the Massachusetts Board of Health, which has just appeared, and in which there is an article on typhoid fever, by a physician of Massachusetts, where again and again there came, from the immediate tainting of a farm-house well, an outbreak of the fever, taking down nearly every person in the house, and resulting in one or two or three deaths in each case. The wells had been in as good condition as yours, but the moment came when they were in a state to receive and multiply the infection, and every man drinking the water fell more or less under the influence of the disease.

Our examination shows, in a few cases, that there are furnaces in the cellars of the houses for heating your rooms, which take their cold air from the cellar. It ought not to be necessary to go into any long argument to prove that a cellar, used as the cellar of any ordinary country-house is, for the storage of provisions, which has very little circulation of air, which is full of dust and impurities, which is more or less the home of rats and mice and cats and dogs, does not contain exactly the sort of atmosphere that you want to warm and bring into your living rooms for your children to breathe during the Winter. I think any one who has had the experience of such cases, or who has investigated the effect of furnace-heated houses upon the health of families, will agree that the fresh air should always be taken entirely from the outside of the house. It is better still, that it should not be taken from near the surface of the ground, the pipe being turned up a few feet to take in a purer air. We have found two, and I think three, cases where drains leading from the kitchen, emptied into the ground. In one case, where there were the ordinary plumbing arrangements, the waste of the whole house passed out through such a drain. We found such cases where the drains passed within a very few feet of the wells, being carried by vitrified pipe, with cemented joints, and supposed to be safe on that account. Now, if the vitrified pipe is sound, which it generally is, and has good joints, which it generally has not, it is safe enough. It has been a part of my work, for many years, to lay these pipes with cement joints, and I have come to the conclusion, that the one great difficulty in draining is, to make a *tight* joint where you are cementing two pipes together. I have almost given it up in despair. There were pipes taken up at Memphis the other day, which I had supposed were absolutely perfect, but my assistant informed me that there was a little stream of water running through in every case. It was very slight, but if it was passing along through the ground near a well, the constant dropping into the soil, not enough perhaps, to go into the well in a stream, but saturating the soil around it, so that when there is a heavy down-pour of rain it might be washed in, it would constitute a dangerous condition. The best remedy is, of course, to lay the pipe to some distance beyond the well, of iron with leaded joints; but where the drain already exists, it is a very easy matter to surround it entirely by a coating of cement concrete that will make it practically tight. Wherever a drain must pass near a well, I strongly advise that course of treatment.

I find another memorandum of a house where the vault is fifteen feet away from the well, is eight feet deep, and is not emptied until nearly full; the well itself being twenty-three feet deep. That case, I think, is very serious. In any community of farmers it would, perhaps, hardly do for a local committee, even if they were so disposed, to treat the hog-pen question as it is treated in cities. We all know that it is absolutely necessary to economical farming and country house-keeping to keep a pig, but it is really not absolutely necessary to keep pigs quite in the condition in which some few are kept in this town. I do not believe the pig is naturally a nasty animal. I don't think he is particularly fond of wallowing in dirty water if he has any other way of cooling himself. I have seen swine kept in a different way, and I would modestly commend to the farmers and housekeepers of this town the suggestion that they learn how pigs may be kept in such a manner that their presence will not be noticed from the house or from the road.

Now, I believe I have stated the chief faults I have been able to find in an examination of nearly every house within this district; and, as you see, I have almost got a harvest of nothing, with the exception of the malarious condition about the mill-pond, due, I believe, entirely to the presence of that pond. With that exception, there is nothing here that is really a justification of my presence in West Ewing.

I shall now be very glad, if any members of my audience choose to ask questions on any sanitary subjects, to answer them to the best of my ability.

Mr. Edward Fisk.—I believe the Secretary has a letter from Prof. Schanck, of Princeton, stating a number of questions, which are quite comprehensive.

Col. Waring.—I will read the letter:

LENOX, MASS., Aug. 25th, 1880.

MY DEAR SIR:—I have not forgotten your request, and only regret that I cannot be present and contribute questions suggested by the occasion and circumstances. I should seek information upon arrangement of grounds, shrubbery, fences, &c., and upon water-closet sewerage and cesspool, &c. Thus:

1. What mixture of grass seed is best for lawns?
2. How often should they be mown?
3. Are door-yard fences needful in a village?
4. Which is the best village hedge material—Arbor Vitæ, Hemlock, &c?
5. For a village without public sewers, which is to be preferred, outside privies, or inside earth closets or water closets?
6. If the latter, how can the efflux be safely disposed of?
7. If a cesspool is uncemented, will it not in time poison the wells?
8. If cemented, will it not fill every few weeks or months, and be a constant nuisance?
9. How should it be trapped and ventilated?

10. What should be done with kitchen slops?

11. Is the Lenox sewerage system applicable to single country houses?

12. In this case, what length of two-inch distributing pipe suffices for each person?

13. May this not freeze up in Winter so as to check distribution?

14. Typhoid fever and kindred diseases are often clearly referable to human excrement, especially when moist and damp. Is the poison introduced through water by stomach, or through air by lungs?

15. What disinfectant is the best for ordinary family use?

16. Relative merits in this respect of air and light, of chlorine, of carbolic acid and of sulphate of iron, also of dry clay.

These are hints and suggestions only, from which you can frame questions and call out information.

Yours very truly,

J. S. SCHANCK.

Col. Waring (quoting from letter.)—"What mixture of grass seed is best for lawns?" [See Notes.]

I would respectfully call on my associate.

Mr. Northrop.—You are familiar with it.

Col. Waring.—Not as familiar as you are. We use Rhode Island bent grass and white clover, introducing a little blue grass seed. I think our best lawns have much white clover.

(Reading again from Prof. Schanck's letter.)—"How often should they be mown?"

My answer to that would be, as often as possible.

(Reading again)—"Are door-yard fences needful in a village?"

Mr. Northrop.—No.

Col. Waring.—Are they *desirable?*

Mr. Northrop.—If you can bring the community to agree, I think they are undesirable. Nothing is more beautiful in a large village, than the absence of fences, and in a farming community like this, where you have the matter entirely under control, it seems to me to promote a sentiment of sociality to have the fences taken away. At Williamstown, Mass., and that model manufacturing village, Cheneyville, at South Manchester, Conn., and the St. Johnsbury factory, in Vermont, and in places where the grounds are thrown together, it adds very much to the general satisfaction.

Col. Waring.—Which is the best village hedge material?

Mr. Northrop.—That depends altogether upon the climate. You cannot give any general direction. There are some places where the osage orange will not grow. It grows here, and very beautifully, if properly cut. [See Notes.]

Col. Waring (reading from the letter.)—"For a village without public sewers, which is to be preferred, outside or inside earth closets, or water closets?"

I should say, where there is land enough about the house to dispose of liquid waste, and where there is water that can be pumped to a supply cistern in the house, that a water closet is much more cleanly and certain of being in good order without extra care, and, therefore, to be preferred. The earth closet is a possible remedy for all evils; but an in-door closet requires, on the part of every person using it, the most constant watchfulness and care, or it becomes offensive. I had to do with the introduction of that improvement in this country, and was its strongest advocate for a very long time. I have no other conveniences in my own house, but I have come slowly to the belief that it is, after all, but a stepping-stone between the old-fashioned arrangement and the well-constructed and well-arranged water closet.

Question by one of the audience:

Dr. Lowrie.—What is the least distance from the house that kitchen and other drainage may properly be disposed of?

Col. Waring.—I will read Prof. Schanck's question on the same subject, in conjunction with this: "How can the efflux be safely disposed of?"

If these matters are to be disposed of by discharging them into cesspools, I should want to put the cesspool to the farthest possible distance—the back field of the farm rather than nearer, for the reason that however well made, and however tightly secured against escape into drinking-water wells, it is really a vast retort filled with foul matter and dangerous gases, which too often find no other means of escape than through the drain to the house. I believe it would be really much better, as a question of health, if the drainage from the house was delivered directly upon the surface of the ground within twenty feet of its back door, bad as this would be, than to have a cesspool at that point. It would not look so well, but I think it would be less dangerous. Fortunately, it is not necessary that either one of these evils should be chosen. A system applicable to every-

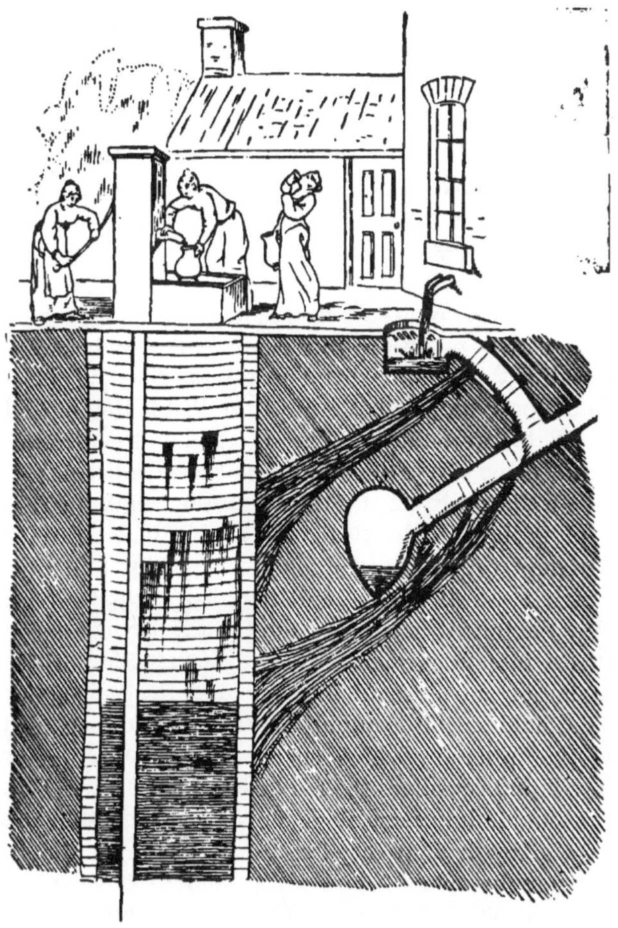

PURE(?) WELL WATER, DEFILED BY DRAINAGE FROM THE KITCHEN SINK AND THE CESSPOOL.
(From "The Sanitary Engineer.")

thing of a liquid character, growing out of an invention made by the inventor of an earth closet in 1868, and since developed by a long experience in England and this country, seems to offer everything that one may desire, if there is a little land around the house. Dr. Lowrie asks within what distance the disposal may take place. I say, always get as far away as you conveniently can. All the liquid waste of my own house is disposed of on a tract of land the first edge of which is about fifteen feet from my piazza, where we spend the Summer. If I had more land, I should go farther away; but with no more land at my disposal I should not hesitate to repeat the same experiment. This system is in use now in a large number of houses in New England and New Jersey, particularly in Orange and in the village of Lenox, from which Prof. Schanck writes, and still more extensively at the Women's prison, at Sherborn, Mass., where there is a very large consumption of water. Its principle is this: That if foul matters are absorbed by the surface soil within reach of the roots of vegetation, and within reach of the atmosphere, the oxygen of which exists in that soil in a state of condensation, they will be acted upon immediately, and will be in a short time completely destroyed; so that if the interval of a day be left between one wetting and another, the action of the roots and of the air will keep the soil always perfectly clean. Suppose we have a drain running down the length of this aisle, made of ordinary drain tiles, and loosely laid at the joints. You attempt to run fifty gallons of sewage through that, and, if the soil is at all porous, and there is a slight leak at every joint, by the time it gets to the other end it has nearly or quite all settled into the ground. Its tendency is to follow the laws of gravitation and descend in the ground, the soil acting as a filter and holding all the impurities behind. Immediately there comes the fresh air, which changes its character or entirely destroys it and consumes the foul matters left there. Now, if it is a question of draining a single house, you have your pipe (we will say a length of twenty-five to fifty feet, according to the character of the soil and slope of the ground,) for each member of the household. It may be one line, or a number of lines branching out from each other, according to the character of the soil. The liquid is delivered into a Field's Flush Tank. When that becomes full, it discharges its whole contents rapidly into the drain. Your tank is arranged to become full once in about two days, so that in every two days there is a rush of water through the drain; its foul waters sink into the soil well filtered, and, by reason of the cleansing action of the air and the roots, the soil is made ready to receive the next accession. In the case of a village, the tank, instead of holding enough for a family for a couple of days, should hold enough for a village a couple of days. In Lenox, the tank holds three thousand gallons, about, and the pipes that receive its discharge are about ten thousand feet in aggregate length. At the prison, the tanks discharge fifteen thousand gallons at a time, and they discharge alternately into two sets of drains of ten thousand feet each; but always working on the same principle, as if you put the water of a single house into a single straight pipe, from which it leaks out into the ground of a door-yard.

Now, as to the result, I can only say that I have never heard of any suspicion of an odor from the surface of the ground under which this operation is taking place. I have never heard of a case of sickness being ascribed to it. I have dug down close to the joints of my own drains, within half an inch of a wide opening which evidently had been receiving copious discharges. and it was impossible to tell, by smell or sight, any difference between that earth and earth taken ten feet away. At the prison, in Massachusetts, our disposal is into artificial draining ground. The whole tract is drained five feet under ground with drains twenty feet apart. The water that is discharged there from the purification of this very foul, black sewage is simply pure water, which I would compare with the well water of any farm-house; at any rate, any village well water, where villages are conducted as they ordinarily are. By chemical analysis it is shown to have a little more organic matter than it ought to have, but it is in such a condition that it is impossible to detect it by anything except a chemical analysis. It is perfectly sweet and clear.

Question.—What you stated as the greatest evil in this town, in a sanitary point of view, was the existence of this mill-dam. I would like to inquire, first, whether the conditions of mill-dams generally are such as to generate this miasma or malaria; and, secondly, whether there is anything special, and what it is, in the condition of this mill-dam which generates disease? You observed that, as a matter of course, it would produce these malarious effects.

Col. Waring.—There is no disadvantage in having a mill-dam, as a mill-dam, if it is simply a reservoir of pure, deep water. If it has steep sides, a change up and down in its elevation can do very little harm; but if, as in this case, the banks are in many places very sloping, and the land is saturated with water for a considerable distance back from its edges, and if, when it is drawn down, a great width of saturated earth is exposed to the sun, or if in parts it is so shallow that the sun's heat will have an effect on the bottom, then the existing conditions are considered to be dangerous, and I have never known them to exist in a country where malaria had a foothold at all, without causing or increasing it.

Question.—If there are, then, pools of standing water which become dried up by drouth, there are similar tendencies?

Col. Waring.—During the time it is passing from the wet to the dry condition. After the ground is dried to a considerable depth, I do not suppose that harm continues; but one of the greatest factors in the generation of malaria is the alternate wetting and drying of land that is subject to malarial poison. Prof. Schanck asks:

"If a cesspool is uncemented, will it not in time poison wells?"

It certainly will, in the cases of wells near enough to it to receive its contents unpurified.

"If cemented, will it not in a few months become a nuisance?"

Yes, if the cement is tight. I imagine that many cesspools get rid of a large quantity of foul water through the imperfection of their work.

"How should it be trapped and ventilated?"

I think, if you have a cesspool, it had better be ventilated as little as possible. If you have a great seething mass, and give it ventilation anywhere within the reach of grounds where you live, there will be great offence from it. I have tried several times to ventilate a cesspool, but I have been compelled to shut it off again. I should rather run drain pipes off through the ground, so that if there were any pressure of air it would work up through the soil, purified in its passage.

Question.—Would you ventilate a cesspool by a chimney?

Col. Waring.—No. Most of the time, if you have a strong upward draft, it is all right; but I never knew a house with such an arrangement that did not at some time have an offensive smell. I believe in ventilating the soil pipe most thoroughly, but not in making it a vent for a foul cesspool. I always run a soil pipe through the roof of the house, and am very careful to place it much lower than any chimney near it.

Question.—In case you had no ventilation to the cesspool, what would you depend upon to prevent the circulation of air to the house?

Col. Waring.—I would have a strong trap in the drain leading to the cesspool; then have air pipes leading from the cesspool out into the soil, so that pressure would be relieved that way.

Question.—What do you think of running a ventilator directly into a chimney that is constantly used for a fire—a kitchen chimney?

Col. Waring.—I do not like it. The fire is not constantly burning. It is not burning at night, and I don't think it is trustworthy. Of course it is better than running into any other chimney.

Question.—What do you think would be the result from that—that the gas might go through from the chimney to the house?

Col. Waring.—I have frequently gone through houses ventilated in that way, which had been unoccupied for two or three days, and the stench from the cesspool was all through the house. Then, frequently, I have found an odor in an upper room through which the chimney passed, which I could trace from no other source than the movement of air through the brick work.

Question.—Suppose you run the ventilator right out across the roof to the chimney?

Col. Waring.—Then you would have danger from the down draft when your kitchen is cold.

Question.—The trap in the closet would not prevent that draft coming in the house?

Col. Waring.—You are ventilating outside of your trap.

Question.—That is what I said. You said it would be a down draft into the house. How could it be?

Col. Waring.—It would be a down draft through the chimney and out through the stove or fire-place.

Question.—What is the width of the lot where you distribute the waste from the house?

Col. Waring.—The main drain is about sixty feet long, and there are nine drains about eighteen or twenty feet each. I have had it in use just ten years. It was put in ten years ago in November.

Question.—Your pipes average about fourteen inches from the surface?

Col. Waring.—Not more than ten or eleven.

Question.—Suppose you have a level surface to distribute it over, where there is scarcely any fall?

Col. Waring.—You need scarcely any. Two inches in a hundred feet is enough, and you can always get that. Within the range at which you can place these pipes, you can always get the fall you need—even if you have to put the pipes a little higher at one end than at the other.

Question.—Can it be worked without a flush tank?

Col. Waring.—It *can* be; but the trouble is, you always keep the ground about the upper end of the pipes saturated, and you have to depend upon the rank vegetation that grows from that excessive moisture.

Question.—You say you have had these drains in use ten years and have not discovered any unpleasant odor arising from the surface?

Col. Waring.—Yes.

Question.—Would that probably be the case ten years hence?

Col. Waring.—I don't think there is the least change in the character of that ground. I think it is exactly the same as it was before I began to use it. I think the oxidization has destroyed all the matter. It may have become a little deeper in color, but, practically, I think it is the same. And the action of this material is so very slight in its reach that while my drains are six feet apart, fully four feet of the space between them shows no effect of the sewerage at all.

Question.—What effect has the frost?

Col. Waring.—I think it has no effect at all. I have had the ground frozen three and one-half feet down, and there was no trouble in my pipes. They have never had any trouble in Lenox. One great point about it is that it is so cheap and simple, and so entirely within the hands of any one who wishes to use it. ·If these poor cottagers down by the canal had these pipes, all they would need would be some place to throw in a bucket of dirty water and that would be their flush tank. [See Col. Waring's Report, on page 42, for further details.]

Col. Waring (reading from letter)—"What disinfectant is the best for ordinary family use?"

Fresh air.

The hour had become too late to discuss all the questions of Prof. Schanck's letter, and, on motion, the meeting was here declared adjourned.

THE
WEST EWING IMPROVEMENT ASSOCIATION.

REPORT ON THE SANITARY CONDITION OF THE WESTERN PART OF EWING TOWNSHIP.

BY COL. GEORGE E. WARING, JR., NEWPORT, R. I.

The examination upon which this report is based, includes an investigation into the character and condition of between forty and fifty dwelling-houses, including the disposal of household wastes and the water supply. No good purpose would be served by detailing in a public report the enumeration of defects of private property. Sufficient notes have been taken concerning each place, and notification is given to the respective owners that on their application, any information which may be desired beyond that of a general character not included in this report, will be cheerfully furnished free of charge.

As a whole, the houses average certainly better than is usual in an agricultural and quarrying district. There is no one of them which might not be very considerably improved by a sufficient expenditure. But I am satisfied that in so far as they or any of them are in a less healthful condition than similar houses in other parts of the country, their defects are chiefly due to two causes:

(1) An improper disposal of liquid and solid household filth including fæcal matter with its attendant fouling of the air, and its contamination of the water supply, and in some cases of the cellars of the houses. In some instances the same difficulty results from the accumulation of the manure of domestic animals in too close proximity to wells or dwellings.

(2) A malarious condition of the site in certain parts of the town, caused by stagnant bays at the side of the canal; by standing water in the quarries; and especially by the damming back of the natural drainage by the dam at Keeler's saw-mill; this latter being far more important, in my judgment, than all other defects combined.

It is not worth while, in making recommendations for the practical improvement of country-houses like those under consideration, to advise the introduction of modern improvements in the way of water supply and drainage, which it would be in some cases beyond the means, and in nearly all cases beyond the inclinations, of the proprietors to adopt. It seems better to confine ourselves to a few simple, practical improvements within easy reach of all, which will constitute in every case a simple and radical improvement over the present conditions, and which will be as much in the way, at present, as it can reasonably be hoped to secure.

The improvement of the ventilation, cleanliness, and, where necessary, of the draining of

CELLARS,

Is certainly very important, and it needs no instruction from me to teach all householders what they already perfectly well understand. It must be evident to all that a wet, close, musty cellar, with no access for fresh air during the Winter time, with accumulations of decaying vegetables and rubbish, is not a good accompaniment of any inhabited house. It is by no means necessary that cellars should be so open to cold winds as to lead to the discomfort of those who live in the rooms above them. But there should certainly be, at all times of the year, a sufficient opportunity for the supply of fresh air to create a sufficient circulation to remove dampness and to carry away the products of the slight inevitable decomposition of what it is necessary to keep in them. A few of the houses within the district are heated by

FURNACES.

These, I believe, with hardly an exception, take their air supply from the cellar. No matter how well ventilated and how clean a cellar may be, its atmosphere is never fit to be heated by the furnace and distributed through the house. It is a very simple, and most important, matter to connect the air supply of the furnace with the outer air by means of a tight wooden box which shall exclude the atmosphere of the cellar from the heated flues.

A CESSPOOL LEACHING INTO A WELL.
(From "The Sanitary Engineer" of July 15, 1879.)

What is not so well understood, or, if understood, is not acted upon, is the absolute importance of

SUNLIGHT AND FRESH AIR.

Let the sun have free access to the outside of the whole house at some time during the day, and keep shutters and blinds and windows open except when it is necessary to exclude it. Never mind faded carpets; they are not so bad as faded cheeks, and these cannot be avoided except by fresh air and ample daylight.

THE DISPOSAL OF HOUSEHOLD WASTES

Is hardly less simple, but it is much less generally understood; and I believe it is safe to say that in nearly every instance where my examinations have been made, the system now adopted is particularly bad. There are very few cases where the well water is not subject to dangerous contamination by the leachings from privy vaults or cesspools or hog-pens or barn-yards, or by the settling into the ground of the drainage from the kitchen sink.

It will be easy, in the matter of hog-pens and barn-yards, to prevent the leachings of their manure from draining toward the well, or from sinking into the ground near the well; and this certainly should be secured, even at the expense of selecting a new site for such deposits, and, so far as possible, by protecting manure from drenching rains. Such protection will be amply repaid by the saving of fertilizing matter which it will secure.

The specific recommendation that I make is, that in every case, whether it be a well-appointed farm-house or simply a laborer's tenement, some means be adopted which will secure an entire abandonment of privy vaults, and a safe disposal of liquid household wasts. These are two distinct items of the work, which may be carried out more or less elaborately according to the means and inclinations of the proprietor. I propose to recommend, in this case, only the simplest and cheapest available methods.

THE PRIVY

Should be removed from its foundation, its vault should be entirely cleaned out, its foundation walls should be removed and the excavation should be continued until clean earth is exposed at every point. It should then be filled to the surface of the ground with clean earth, and, if it is necessary to use the same site in future, this should be so rammed in the filling as to prevent future settling. It will be better, in all cases, to remove the building at least far enough to secure a sound foundation. The building should then be set on posts or piers so that the lower side of its sill shall be at least eighteen inches above the surface of the ground; suitable steps being constructed for its approach. Lay on the ground, with cross-stays to hold

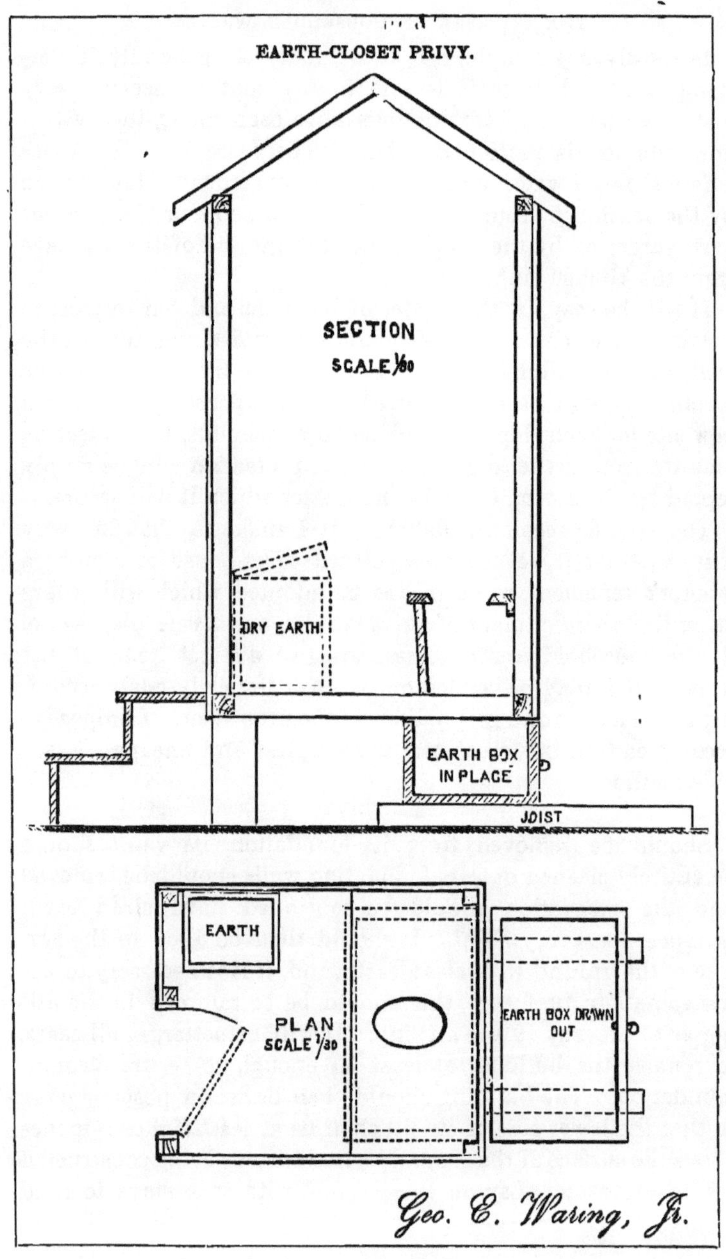
EARTH-CLOSET PRIVY.
SECTION
SCALE 1/30
DRY EARTH
EARTH BOX
IN PLACE
JOIST
EARTH
PLAN
SCALE 1/30
EARTH BOX DRAWN
OUT
Geo. E. Waring, Jr.

them in position, two joists extending at least from the front of the seat to two feet outside of the building, at the rear.

Make a box of stout planks to rest upon these joists, large enough to reach well under the seat and high enough barely to pass the sill easily. Secure a stout handle to this box by which it may be drawn out over the joists outside when necessary for emptying. The inside of the box should be well rendered with hot coal tar quite to the top. This is the receptacle for fæcal matter. Its bottom should be covered at least to the depth of one inch with dry earth or ashes. In the house there should be a second box containing dry earth or screened ashes, and a hand scoop should be furnished with which to throw it into the box below. After each use of the privy, rather more than a pint of this material should be thrown down to cover the dejections and and to absorb the urine. From time to time it will be necessary to rake down or level off the accumulations, and when the box becomes full it should be drawn out and emptied, its contents being used as manure. This constitutes the cheapest form of earth closet; and it secures, if care is given to the uniform covering of the deposits, a perfect suppression of odor, and entire prevention of injurious decomposition, and a perfectly healthy and satisfactory condition. The value of the manure will be quite sufficient to compensate for the slight additional trouble; and the avoiding of the horrible stench of the usual country privy will secure the great difference between a brutal filthiness and civilized decency. Those who desire something more elaborate and more convenient in its operation, may address "Earth Closet Company, Hartford, Conn.," for the mechanical apparatus by which the deposit of earth is made automatic.

THE DISPOSAL OF KITCHEN SINK WASTE,

Chamber slops and laundry water, is a question which has engaged the study and ingenuity of the world for many years. I believe that, so far as isolated country-houses are concerned, it has been perfectly accomplished by the system known as "sub-surface irrigation." This system is susceptible of much elaboration, and may be carried out in an expensive manner; but its essential results may be secured with an expense so trifling that not even in the smallest tenement-house need its cost be an obstacle to

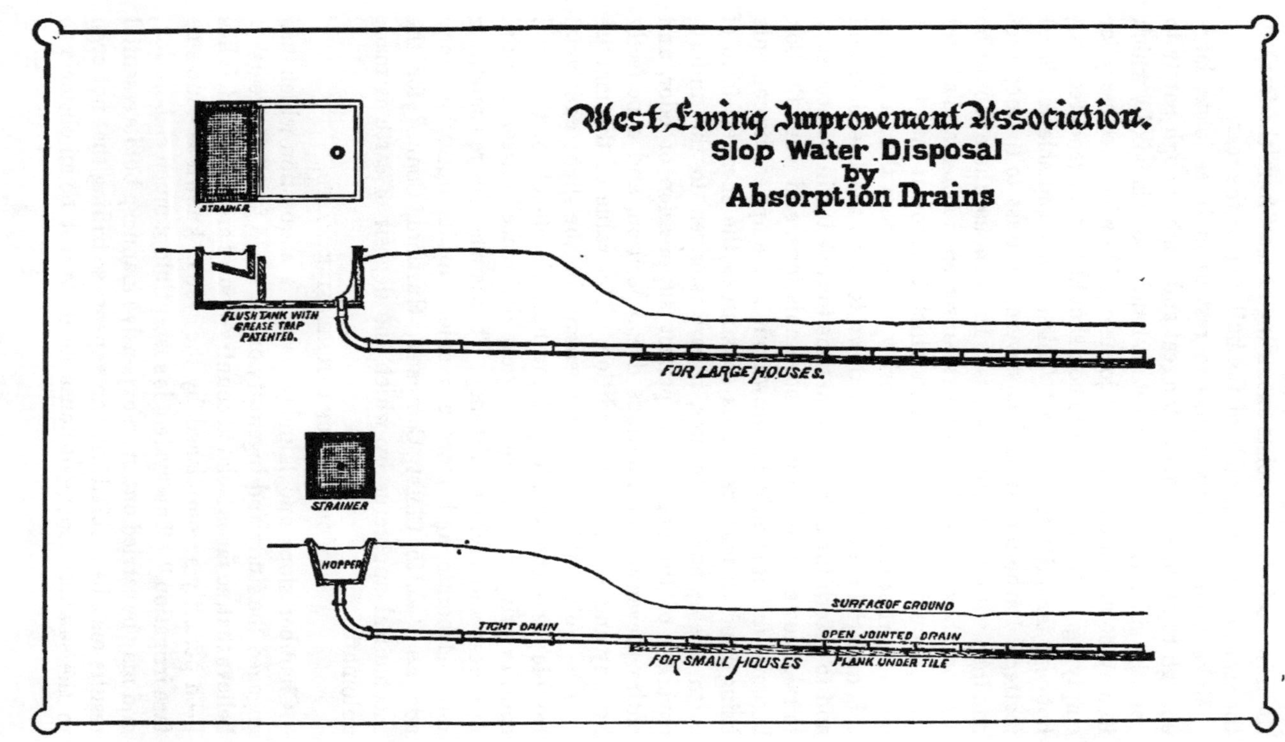
West Ewing Improvement Association.
Slop Water Disposal
by
Absorption Drains
STRAINER
FLUSH TANK WITH GREASE TRAP PATENTED.
FOR LARGE HOUSES.
STRAINER
HOPPER
TIGHT DRAIN
SURFACE OF GROUND
OPEN JOINTED DRAIN
FOR SMALL HOUSES
PLANK UNDER TILE

its adoption. It is based on the fact that the surface soil which is within the reach of the roots of grass or other plants, and of the action of the atmosphere, is a very active destroyer of organic matter. A cotton rag buried a few inches under the surface is very soon entirely consumed by this action; and all decomposable matter so placed is destroyed by oxidation or slow combustion as completely, though less rapidly, as when it is thrown into the fire. In order to make this process continuous, it is necessary that there should be free access of air into the pores of the soil. In the case of liquid wastes, it is necessary that the discharge be intermittent, for when a constant small stream runs into the ground, saturating a small area, the entrance of the air is prevented and the oxidizing action is retarded. With even a few hours' interval between the two discharges, the water settles away into the ground, which acts as a filter, holding back all of its impurities, and its descent is followed by the entrance of fresh air, which immediately attacks and destroys the retained organic matter. If the liquid is thrown on the top of the ground, it produces in a short time a fuddled condition of the surface which prevents the free entrance of air. It is, therefore, desirable to introduce it into the soil below the surface, allowing it to soak away in so gradual a manner that no fuddling of the earth can take place. This introduction into the earth is by the use of common agricultural drain tiles with open joints, laid not more than ten inches below the surface. The intermittent action is secured by delivering liquid wastes into these tiles, not constantly, but from time to time.

In the case of a small tenement-house, where only two or three pailfuls of waste liquid are produced in the course of the day, this absorption drain need not be more than forty feet long. It may be one continuous line of pipe, or it may be several shorter pipes branching from one main line, according to the space devoted to the use. It may lie under the grass near a row of currant bushes, under a grape-vine trellis, under a grass plat, or elsewhere. Opening into it, there should be a box [See cut on page 48] large enough to hold a pailful of water; and the joints of this box, as well as the space around the pipe leading from it, should be made tight. It may be covered in Winter, as a protection against frost; but in Summer it will be better that it should have a full exposure to the air. A wire cloth or other screen should be provided at its top to act as a strainer to hold back coarse matters which might obstruct the pipe. From time to time, this strainer, which should be movable, can be emptied into the swill barrel, or its contents may be thrown upon the manure heap, or buried in the ground. The liquid which passes the strainer will enter the pipe, leach out into the ground and be purified. The arrangement described will be quite sufficient to receive the contents of one or two wash tubs; but it should not be connected with the kitchen sink delivering only a small flow. Whatever is thrown into it should go with a rush, so as to reach as far as possible through the whole length of the drains.

For houses of larger size, producing a greater amount of waste, the length of drain should be from one hundred and fifty to three hundred feet, including all branches, according to the size of the family and the freedom with which water is used. A uniform distribution through this length of pipe cannot be secured by throwing into it a pailful at a time. Some arrangement should be adopted which will retain water to the amount of a barrelful or more, and which will, when the tank becomes full, deliver the whole contents suddenly. The apparatus best adapted for this use is known as "Field's Flush Tank," which is made of cast iron, and which is sold for about thirty dollars, by A. G. Myers, 94 Beekman street, New York. A much cheaper arrangement can be made at home, which, while not having the advantage of the Field automatic siphon, will secure the same result, if attention is given to opening and closing its outlet by hand. The construction of this tank is shown on page 48. It is made of plank, and is separated by a grease-catcher, which will prevent congealed grease, floating substances and heavy matters from passing into the discharging chamber. It also has a spatter-board, to prevent the disturbance of the sediment, and a screen to hold back coarse matters. It is, in fact, a flushing tank with a grease-trap intervening between it and the source of supply. This interposition of a grease-trap

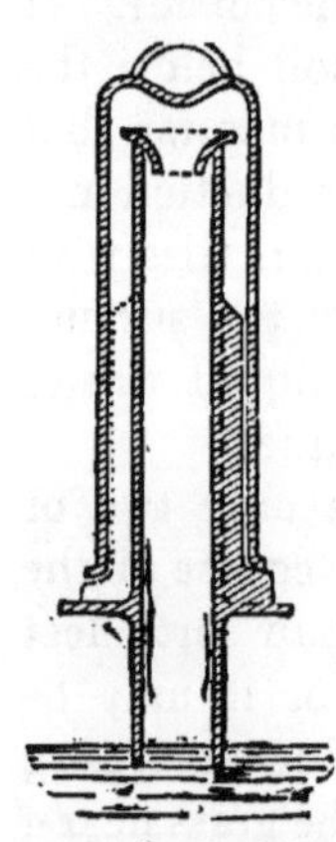

FIELD'S PATENT ANNULAR SIPHON.

is covered by a patent of my own; but permission is hereby given to any member of the West Ewing Improvement Association to use it, without charge. The size of tank indicated in the sketch is sufficient for three hundred feet of drain. The capacity of its second or discharging chamber may be proportionately reduced or increased as the length of drain is made greater or less. The grease-trap may be attached to any waste-pipe from the house, or it may be filled by pouring into it the

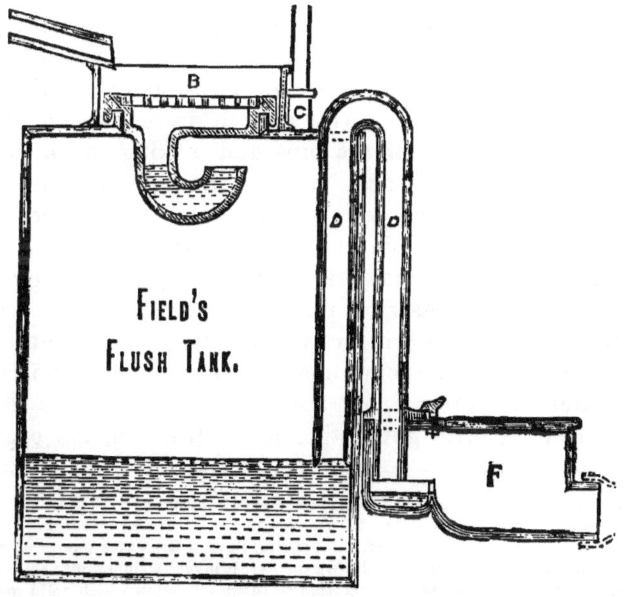

contents of chamber pails, wash tubs, slop pails, &c. The grease-trap serves to hold back all obstructing matters. The outlet of the discharging chamber is closed by a plug of wood,

---

Description of Field's Flush Tank.—It is intended to be placed immediately outside of the walls of the house, and to receive all of its liquid wastes. It is made entirely of earthenware or of cast iron. The liquids pass through the grating of the pan (B), and are discharged through a trap which prevents the contained air of the tank from escaping. (C) is a socket for a ventilating pipe to carry this contained air to the top of the house. The tank holds about 20 or 30 gallons. This has no outlet save through the siphon (D). The outer end of the siphon enters a discharging trough (F), which is made to turn to the right or left, so that its mouth may be directed as required to connect the tank with the line of outlet pipes. This trough is of a peculiar shape which assists small quantities of liquid in bringing the siphon into action,

or by an india rubber ball; the stopper being attached to a chain, by which it may be lifted whenever the discharging chamber becomes full. After the chamber has discharged itself, this outlet should be tightly closed. To make this arrangement automatic in its working, it is only necessary to substitute for the plug, the Field's Patent Siphon shown on page 50.

A little judgment will be necessary in adjusting this apparatus to the lay of the land. If the absorption ground is to be placed at some distance from the house—and it should never be nearer than fifteen feet to any well from which drinking water is taken —it may be connected with the flush tank by a vitrified pipe with very securely-cemented joints. These joints should first be packed with oakum, or with rags, to prevent cement from running to the inside of the pipe and making rough points to arrest foreign substances passing through to them, and they should be covered with a good band of the very best hydraulic cement—the joints not being covered with earth until it is quite certain that they are absolutely tight. This precaution is especially necessary in passing near a well. The absorption tiles should be two inches in diameter, and only one foot long, in order that the joints may be frequent. Their form is not of much importance, but the best material for the use is the round pipes with gutter tiles to lay them in, and caps to

---

instead of merely dribbling over the siphon without charging it as they otherwise would do, and has a cover which can be removed to give access for cleaning.

When the tank is entirely filled, the pouring in of a few extra quarts of water, which is sure to occur at some time during the day, brings the siphon into action, and it flows copiously until the tank is emptied to the depth below which solid matters are permitted to accumulate, to be occasionally cleared out on removing the pan (B).

As the sink pipe discharges over the grating of the trapped inlet (B) outside the house, the connection between the drains and the house is completely broken, and any entry of foul air from the drain is rendered impossible. The top of the tank is perfectly closed by means of the water joint around the cover, and the cover is readily removed when required. The inlet, moreover, forms a basin, which may be used for throwing down slops outside the house.

When used for the *disposal of house slops where no regular system of sewerage exists*, the flush tank enables all house refuse to be removed inoffensively—the bed-room slops being thrown down the basin at the top of the tank outside the house—and thus where earth or other dry closets are used for the excreta, this apparatus supplies a complete sanitary system of drainage. The concentration of the flow of the sewage effected by the sudden discharge of the tanks, forces the liquid rapidly along the pipes, and prevents their being choked. The liquid can thus be distributed over a sufficient area of ground to give full opportunity for the soil to purify it. The tanks are ordinarily made to contain 20 or 30 gallons in addition to space for deposit.

keep the dirt from entering the joints from above, manufactured by C. W. Boynton, Woodbridge, N. J. The joints must not be too tight. If the gutters are not used, the tiles should be laid on strips of board, for it is now and then necessary to remove some portion of the drain to clear out accumulations, and either the gutters or the strips are desirable to secure their being relaid on the proper grade. The grade or pitch of these drains should not be too rapid, lest the water flow too much to the far end

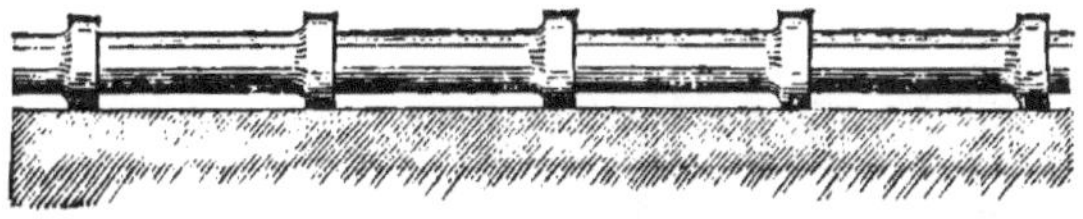

PIPES RESTING ON THEIR SHOULDERS.

THE IMPROPER WAY TO LAY THE VITRIFIED PIPE.

and force its way up to the surface of the ground. It has been found in practice that four inches fall, or, at the utmost, six inches fall in one hundred feet, is better than anything steeper. If the land slopes more than this, the tiles should be laid obliquely across the slope. If the yard or garden where the disposal is to be made is on the same level with the house, the tank will have to be built considerably out of ground. If the ground about the house is higher than that used for disposal, it

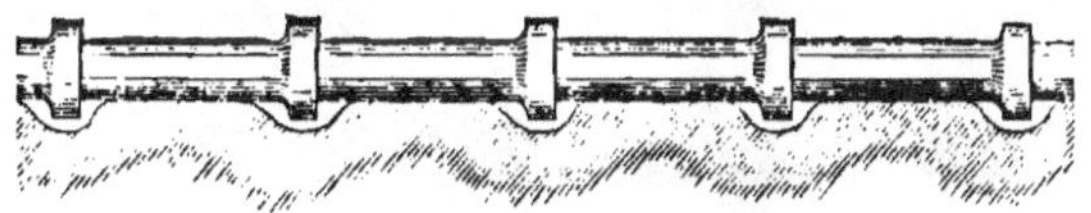

PIPES RESTING ON THEIR FULL LENGTH.

THE PROPER WAY TO LAY THE VITRIFIED PIPE.

may be built entirely in the ground. In this latter case, the cemented pipe will be enough below the surface to prevent its disturbance by frost. If these joints must be within eighteen inches or less of the surface of the ground, the course of the tight part of the drain should be covered with litter during the Winter season; and in this case, as well as in that of the one referred to above, the tank itself should be protected against frost. Its contents will be so warm that a little covering will be sufficient.

I repeat that I am disposed to confine my general recommendations to these two general improvements. If their general adoption can be secured, the Association will have accomplished a result which cannot fail to have the most advantageous influence upon the health of the community, and, I am disposed to say, upon the self-respect and comfort of its members.

RATS AND THE TALE THEY TELL.
(From "The Sanitary Engineer" of July 15, 1879.)

THE BAYS AT THE SIDE OF THE CANAL

Or feeder are in many places too shallow. Wherever malaria has gained a foot-hold, as it certainly has in this vicinity, shallow, stagnant water should be avoided. Every pond or bay should be deep enough to be sufficiently beyond the influence of the sun's heat to prevent vegetation at the bottom. The banks of these bays and of all ponds should be steep, and they should be grassed to the waters edge. If there is any material variation in the level of water in the canal, by which its edges are made alternately wet and dry, this condition must be overcome, or the people must accept the fact that they live in the presence of a source of malaria which they cannot remove. It may be a great source of malaria or it may be slight. It certainly is incomparably less than the difficulty caused by

KEELER'S MILL-DAM.

This dam I consider by far the most serious factor, so far as malaria is concerned, with which we have to deal. Its bad influence is felt all the way from the mill up to the rear of the River Bend estate, and as much farther as the wind is capable of bearing the malarial influence.

The whole question of malaria is imperfectly understood, and we can reason about it only from ascertained general principles; but some of these are so well demonstrated that no sanitarian would presume to disregard them. Two different conditions are acknowledged to be of the very worst character. They are:

(1) The complete saturation of the ground within a short distance of the surface, that surface being exposed to the action of the sun.

(2) The raising and lowering of the levels of bodies of water so that their shores are alternately wet and dry.

Both of these conditions are secured in the most complete manner in the case in question. Much of the land bordering the brook and its enlargements, which constitute Keeler's mill-pond, and which extend for nearly a mile along the west side of the canal, is so low as to be completely saturated by the water of that brook. The supplies of this stream are so insignificant in amount that they can count as very little against the draft upon the pond when the mill is in operation. The water is drawn off much more rapidly than it flows in, and it exposes wide stretches of bank to the action of the sun.

No doubt some difficulty comes from the stagnation of water in the quarries, and still more, perhaps, from the leaking of the canal. It is possible, too, that the draining between Keeler's pond and the water-power is less effective than it should be. But all these may be overcome if the dam is removed; and all combined are insignificant as compared with the pond, which, in my opinion, constitutes a nuisance of such magnitude that the community cannot safely permit it to continue.

That there results from the sources that I have indicated, a very serious malarial condition which is producing a disastrous effect upon the people who live in this vicinity, is fully demonstrated by an investigation recently made by Rev. Dr. Lowrie.

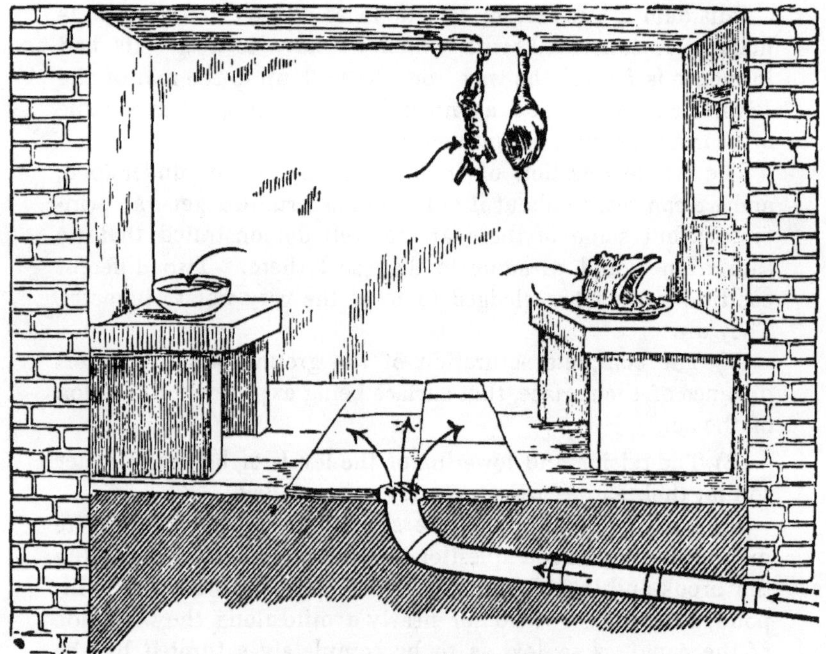

MILK AND PROVISION ROOM WITH UNTRAPPED SINK.
(From "The Sanitary Engineer.")

This investigation relates to twenty-three families, being all the households beginning with his own and proceeding up the Greensburg road, and at the quarries immediately about the Greensburg railroad station. The inquiries related to chills and fever during the Spring and Summer up to the middle of July. At this latter date there were only three households in which the disease did not exist at the time, and one of these three had had it in the Spring. The total number of cases was fifty-one.

Dr. Lowrie very truly says: "Fifty-one cases of chills and fever in a total of twenty-three families is the expression of no small amount of misery."

Obviously there are no means by which the difficulty caused by the overflowing and saturation of the land by the mill-dam can be obviated without injury to the water-power. Therefore the simplest way to overcome it is the best way. The first step to be taken is to extinguish the mill right, and to remove the dam entirely, giving the brook for its whole length up to and through Mr. Fisk's estate a deep, clean and permanent channel. It would be better even that, wherever practicable, its bed should be at least four feet below the level of its immediate banks; the banks having a slope of two horizontal to one perpendicular, and being grassed.

I have been asked to give plans and estimates of the cost of this work, but I find that it would be impossible to do so even approximately, without a more careful survey of the ground than I have been able to make. Certainly the cost need not be considerable, and it can bear no comparison to the value of the result to be secured.

NOTES.

The Proper Treatment of Deciduous Hedges, and in particular of the Maclura or Osage Orange.

I. PREPARATION OF THE HEDGE ROW.

The ground should be in good condition, *i. e.*, dry enough and mellow enough to raise a good crop of corn. Spouty lands should be drained; low, wet places may be filled up by ditching, on either or both sides, raising an embankment, which should be fully eight feet wide. This may be done by the plow alone, or by using the scraper also, where horses can be worked, otherwise the spade must be resorted to.

Have your line surveyed before preparing it; find exactly where you want the hedge to stand, put a tall stake at each end, and perhaps several between, if it is a long line; plow first *out from the row on both sides* [See Fig. 1], then finish by *back furrow-*

FIG. 1.

ing, so as to leave the row a trifle higher than the surrounding surface, to throw off standing water. Harrow and roll the ground well, and set stakes in a straight line with those at the ends, every five rods. Stretch a line of cotton cord, six inches to one side of these stakes, for a guide in setting the plants.

II. SETTING THE PLANTS.

This should be done in the Spring. Prepare the plant for setting, by thinning off all side roots, and cutting back the main root to about eight inches in length. The plants may be set in various ways, either by the use of the spade, dibble or trowel. The plan recommended by Warder, in his "Hedges and Evergreens," as being most sure of success and most rapid, is "to stretch a line upon the course of the future hedge, on the mellow and well-prepared soil; then a *clean* spade is pressed deeply into the ground, the blade being in a vertical direction and close to the line; pushing the handle from you, a crack is opened to the depth of the instrument; into this the little plant is inserted with the left hand, and retained in its position while the spade is withdrawn, and until it is turned with its face toward the operator and again inserted, at a distance of three inches from the first cut, in such a direction that, when pressed home, the edge shall reach the point of the first cut, near the place occupied by the root of the plant, where it is to be drawn firmly toward the operator, to fix the plant in its place. This operation

FIG. 2.—SHOWING THE YOUNG PLANT SET IN THE ROW.

is rapid and very simple; in its first introduction, the blade is to be perpendicular or vertical, with its back toward you; in the second, the *handle* is to be upright, and the cavity of the blade should be held toward the digger. The distance may be regulated by the eye, and a little practice will give sufficient accuracy."

Avoid two serious errors, viz.: (1) Crowding the row too near a fence, and (2) setting the plants too close in the row. Five feet is the least distance which the row should be planted from a fence, and the plants should not be set closer together than twelve, and, preferably, eighteen inches.

III. CULTURE DURING THE FIRST YEAR.

For the first year or two the main object is to make good roots. To that end do not trim the hedge any the first year. Keep the hedge row clean by frequent cultivation, just as you would a row of corn, and late in the Fall plow two rather heavy furrows to the row, forming a ridge about it to protect the roots; for if the tops be frozen, it is no matter, as they are to be cut off the following Spring.

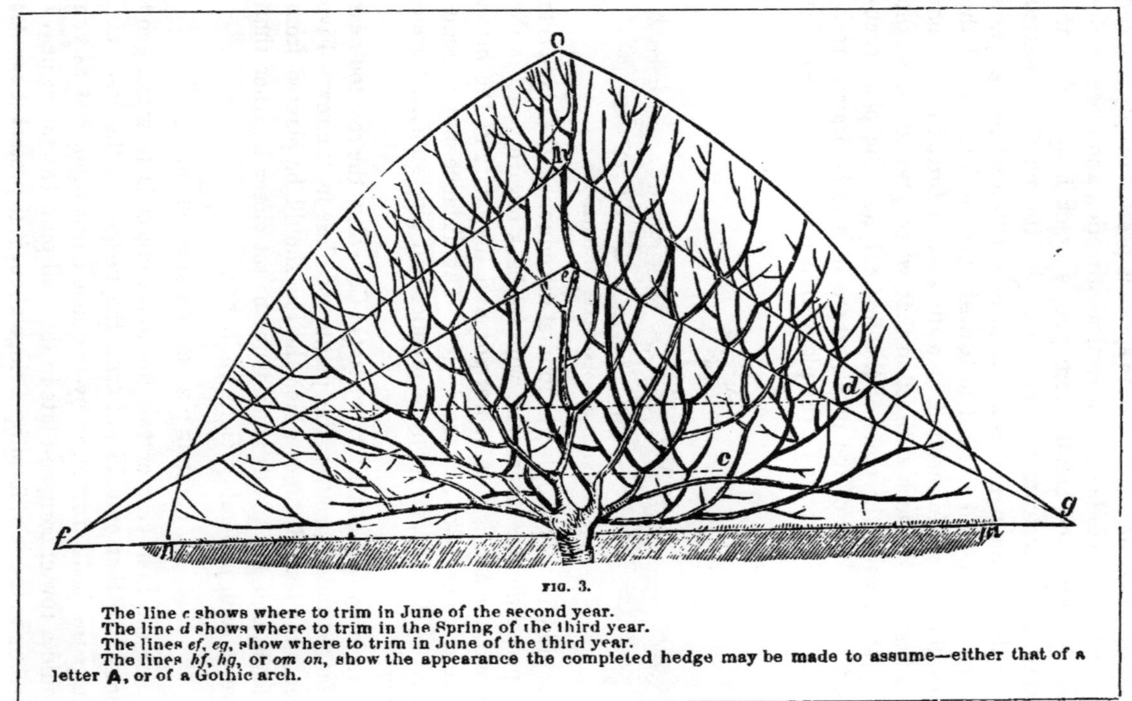

FIG. 3.

The line *c* shows where to trim in June of the second year.
The line *d* shows where to trim in the Spring of the third year.
The lines *ef*, *eg*, show where to trim in June of the third year.
The lines *hf*, *hg*, or *om on*, show the appearance the completed hedge may be made to assume—either that of a letter **A**, or of a Gothic arch.

IV. CULTURE DURING THE SECOND AND SUCCEEDING YEARS.

A most important duty in the second Spring is to replace all dead or sickly plants with new, strong plants, cutting off the tops of the replants as they are set out.

The culture of the hedge the second season should be carefully attended to and the ground frequently stirred with the plow or cultivator, followed by the hoe when necessary. The following directions for trimming should be closely followed:

In the *Spring* of the second year, the whole of the wood is to be removed, by cutting off at the ground, with the scythe or mowing machine.

In June of the same year, or so soon as the multitude of shoots that will have made their appearance have become sufficiently woody to bear the knife, they are to be cut off at four inches from the ground (See Fig. 3). This will reduce the hedge to a low level, although the horizontal branches may spread over one or two feet, or more in width. No disturbance of the lateral shoots should be allowed, as they are wanted to give breadth to the future hedge; and *unless the bottom is provided at first, it can never be afterward supplied.*

The line *d* in the illustration shows the place for the cut to be made in trimming with the scythe in the Spring of the third year. The Summer pruning should be again performed in June, and should follow the lines *e f* and *e g* of the illustration, for now we must begin to give the hedge its proper form. The end view of a properly trimmed hedge should present the appearance of letter **A**. This shape secures to every leaf and twig the benefit of all the sunshine, air, rain or dew, that it is possible for it to receive.

Again, in August, the hedge should be trimmed, being careful to preserve the pyramidal form. These trimmings need not be so close as when we were forming the base. Six inches will do very well.

The trimming of subsequent years should be kept up on the same principle, being careful to preserve the slope of the sides which will gradually become more precipitous as years go by, but which must never be allowed to assume the perpendicular form.—[*Condensed from Warder's "Hedges and Evergreens," published by the Orange Judd Company,* 245 *Broadway, New York.*

Sidewalks and Roadways.—How to Make Them and How to Take Care of Them.

I. SIDEWALKS.

No one thing has more to do with the comfort of those living in the country, than sidewalks which are good at all seasons of the year.

To overcome occasional sloppiness where the difficulty is not deep-seated, there is no cheaper nor better device than to dress the surface with coal ashes. Indeed, if these are used to a sufficient thickness, they are practically as good as concrete or the best gravel. When first applied, they are dusty and unpleasant; but the first wetting lays the dust, and they soon settle to a firm

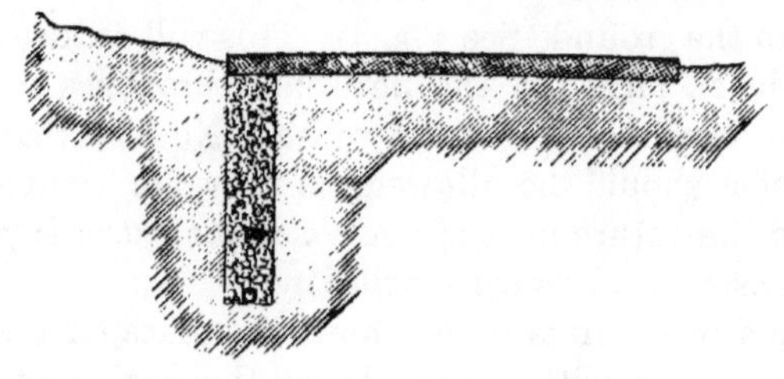

FIG. I.

consistency and make a very pleasant walk, with the great advantage of being entirely barren, and preventing the growth of weeds and grass.

It is a common impression, that all thoroughly good foot-paths must be dug out to a considerable depth, filled with loose stones, and dressed at the top with some good finishing material; but this is not necessary even for the best work. The great point is to secure a thorough draining of the sub-stratum, so that there shall be no rising of ooze-water from below, and so that the ground shall be free from such saturation as to cause heaving during frost. This condition may be secured by a suitable draining of the ground immediately under the walk, and by the use of a well-compacted and tightly-bound surface covering of such form as to shed or turn away rain water. Figure 1 shows the cross-section of a foot-path six feet wide, on slightly sloping ground, where we have to apprehend an oozing of subsoil water from the land at the highest side. The center of the walk is slightly crowning,—say one inch higher than the sides,—so that rain falling upon it will flow readily toward the grass border at either side. To prevent the ponding of water at the sides when the ground is frozen, the surface of the walk at its edges should be well above the level of the adjoining ground; but it may be necessary under some circumstances to furnish, here and there, a channel or surface gutter across the walk, to allow the accumulation at the higher side to escape. Rarely will deep gutters at the sides be necessary or desirable. We will assume that the path in question is to be made over a tenacious clay soil, with a considerable oozing from the hill-side,—the most unfavorable condition that can be found, especially in cold climates. The first thing to be secured is the cutting off of the subsoil water from the hill. This may be done by digging a trench as narrow as possible—six inches will be better than more, as requiring less filling material—to a depth of three feet. In the bottom of this drain lay a common land-tile drain, with collars at the joints, if these can be procured, and, if not, with a bit of paper laid over the joints to prevent the entrance of loose material, and to hold the pipes in place during construction. The ditch should then be filled with cinders, gravel, or coarse sand. If stones are to be used, they should be broken to a small size—not more than one inch in diameter—and the loose bits should be mixed with them in the filling. Very small interstices will be sufficient to allow water to pass freely through, while if large stones are used, with large interstices, there will be danger of a washing in of earth sufficient in time to obstruct both the stone work and the tile. The smaller the tile, so long as it is sufficient for its purpose, the better; for lengths of five hundred feet or less, an interior diameter of an inch and a quarter will be sufficient; from this to one thousand feet, use an inch and a half bore. If possible, before exceeding this length, secure an outlet for the water in the road-side gutter or some other channel of exit. The tile drain, at a depth of three feet, will remove all subsoil water from under the walk and all that may be delivered into the loosely-filled trench at its side. The loose filling of the trench should not be carried nearer than within six inches of the surface of the ground, and should be covered with fine and well-packed earth to prevent the entrance of *surface* water which would soon carry in silt enough to stop its action. Whatever covering is adopted for the walk itself, it must be of such a character as to prevent anything like a free admission of surface water. Concrete will do this perfectly; and either ashes, or gravel dressed at the top with ashes, if well raked and rolled at the outset to a smooth surface, will soon become so bound together as to shed pretty nearly all rain falling upon it. The difference in cost between a walk made in this way, and one dug out for its whole width to a depth of two feet, and filled first with stone and then with gravel and a suitable surface dressing, will be very important; and it is safe to say that the cheaper will be at least as good and durable as the more expensive method.

II. ROADWAYS.

The great expense of macadamizing or telfordizing puts these systems almost out of the reach of small communities. Wherever the original expense can be borne, the subsequent cost of maintenance will be so slight, and the result generally will be so satisfactory, as to make it always a good investment. The circumstances under which these costly forms of construction may be adopted will be greatly extended if we can overcome the prevalent American prejudice in favor of *wide* roadways.

Under most circumstances twenty feet of roadway will be ample. This will allow the moving of three vehicles side by side, and will give a leeway of six feet between two vehicles passing each other.

On both sides of this roadway, except for the necessary sidewalks, the whole space to the fences should be in well-kept grass, which is the cheapest to secure, the most economical to maintain, and the most agreeable to see, of all ground covering.

In considering the width to be given to roadways, it should be understood that every form of road is more or less costly to make and keep in order, and that the cost of both items is in direct proportion to the width. If to the cost of making and grading an ordinary roadway sixty feet wide, we add the capital sum whose interest would be necessary to keep this width in good repair, we shall have an amount that would go far toward the construction and maintenance of a road of the very best quality only thirty feet wide. Furthermore, while it is impossible to estimate such items exactly, and while the amount thus saved cannot be controlled for the road-making account, the saving in the wear and tear of vehicles, and in the team force needed to move heavy loads, constitutes an important argument in favor of the best construction. The amount thus saved in the short streets of villages, where the principal traffic is over rough country roads, would not be very great, but it would enable the road authorities of the township to realize the advantage of first-rate roads and the degree to which the narrowing of the roadway cheapens construction. As a result, there would soon be an extension of the improvement over the more important highways into the country, where a well-metalled width of twelve feet would accommodate nearly the whole traffic, and where the proper application of a cheap system of under-drainage would make well-metalled roads extremely cheap to maintain.

In the island of Jersey, there are many excellent roads only six feet wide. These are provided with frequent little bays or turn-outs to allow teams to pass each other. Although such extremely narrow roads are not to be recommended, the difference in comfort and economy of team-power between these and the average American dirt road is enormously in their favor. The widest roads in Jersey, leading from a busy town of thirty thousand inhabitants into a thickly-settled farming region where business and pleasure travel is very active, and where "excursion cars" carrying thirty or forty persons are constantly passing, are only twenty-four feet wide; often only of this width between the hedge-rows, the road itself being an excellent foot-path for its whole width. Nowhere else in the world is the rural charm more perfectly developed than in Jersey, and no element of its great beauty is so conspicuous and so constantly satisfactory as its narrow and embowered lanes and roadways.

The great enemy of all roads is excessive moisture; and the chief purpose of all methods of improvement is to get rid of this, or to counteract its effect. As in the case of foot-paths, wherever the porous character of the subsoil, and the absence of higher-lying wet lands, is such that no accumulation of water upon or under the roadway need be feared, the greatest difficulty is at once set aside.

Where such natural drainage is secured, no artificial underdrainage will be needed. In many more instances, all that will be required in the way of draining will be to lead away the sources of wet-weather springs, which break through the roadbed and cause deep sloughs. Where incomplete or partial artificial under-draining is needed, the need is absolute; and whether we consider the durability of the road, or the degree to which its traffic is interfered with by its wet condition, we may be confident that every dollar spent in well-directed under-draining will be invested to the very best advantage.

If the trouble is local, here and there in spots, and is obviously caused by the breaking up of springs from the road-bed, such partial work may be adopted as will tap the sources of these springs, and lead their water harmlessly away. Gisborne, one of the best agricultural writers of England, put the case tersely and well when—objecting to the system of circumventing springs—he said "*Hit him straight in the eye*, is as good a maxim in draining as in pugilism." It is best not to pass up at the side of a spring, and so creep around behind it to head off its water; but to drive the drain straight through it, and far enough beyond it to tap and lead away at a lower level the water which causes it. These drains, as well as all others intended simply to remove subsoil water, and not to cut off a weeping stream, are best made with common drain-tiles laid as before directed, and covered immediately with well-packed earth. Water enters an under-drain, not from above, but from below; that is to say, as water, from whatever source, fills the subsoil, it rises therein until it reaches the floor of the drain, when it enters and is led away, just as water falling into a cask which stands on end flows off at the under side of the bung-hole when it reaches its level. Even if the cask be filled to the top with earth, the rain falling upon it will descend perpendicularly to the bottom, and will flow off at the bung only when the soil to that level has become saturated. It will descend through the soil by the straightest course, and will raise the general level. It will not violate the laws of gravitation, and run diagonally toward the point of outlet, as seems to be the general supposition when the perplexing question, "How does water get into the drain?" is first considered. When we drive a drain through a spring and into the water-bearing stratum which feeds it, we simply make it easier for the water to escape by the drain than to keep on at the higher level, and break out at the surface of the ground.

As in the case of the sidewalks illustrated in Figure 1, in cutting off a continuous weeping or ooze from higher land, it is best to introduce a vertical filling of porous material through which the water will descend and enter the drain; but, excepting this single instance, all that we need to do, so for as subterranean work is concerned, is to furnish an easy and sufficient channel for the removal of subsoil water.

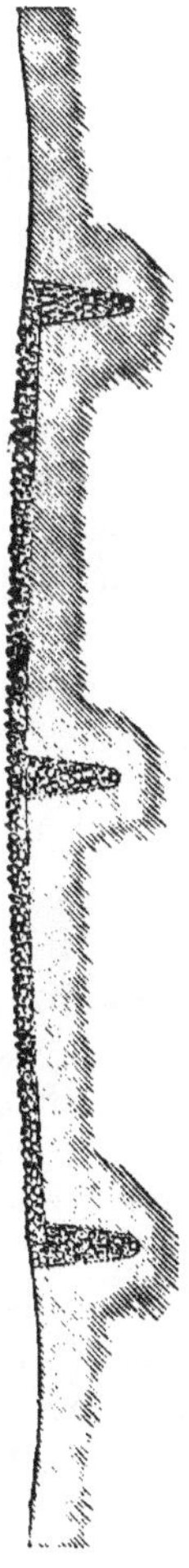

What constitutes a sufficient drain is something very much less than what is generally supposed. In ordinary agricultural drainage, where the lines of tiles are forty feet apart, a well-laid tile an inch and a quarter in diameter is sufficient for a length of one thousand feet—that is, it is sufficient to remove the water of filtration from an acre of land. If laid with only an inclination of six inches in one hundred feet, its delivery will be so rapid as to amount to more than a heavy, continuous rainfall upon this area. In road drainage, the same rule would hold true; but, as the soil offers a certain resistance to the rapid descent of water, it is best to give a means of outlet at smaller intervals; and for the best work in roads thirty feet wide or more, three drains could be used with advantage. In no case, however, need the size of pipes be larger than above indicated, if the form of the tiles is true, and if they are well joined together at their ends.

Fig. 2.

Figure 2 shows the cross-section of a country road thirty feet wide, with three lines of tile-drain laid at a depth of about three feet below it. Except in case of necessity, these drains should have an inclination of not less than six inches in one hundred feet. There is no objection to their having more than this wherever the lay of the land permits or requires it. They may often have considerably less in case of need; but, the smaller the rate of inclination, the greater the care needed in securing a true grade. The water of these drains should be collected into a single drain, and led away at intervals of from five hundred to one thousand feet. It may be delivered into a road-side gutter, or into a collecting underdrain, according to the requirements of the situation.

The removal of excessive subsoil moisture being secured, attention should next be given to the surface of the road, which should be finished with the firmest material at hand—with the common earth of the subsoil where nothing better can be afforded—and which should be brought to a true grade, with a *very slight* slope from the center to the edge. For a road thirty feet wide, the elevation of the center above the level of the edges should not be more than four or six inches, and the grade should be made on a straight line rather than on a curve. If the road is made as flat as the turning-off of surface-water will permit, it will be traveled upon in all its parts; while if it is crowned to a high arch, as is often the case, it will soon be found that the best place to drive is in the middle of the road, and foot-tracks and wheel-tracks will soon form slight channels or ruts which will lead water lengthwise along the road, and which will cause an undue amount of wear and washing. A road may be actually flat to the eye, and equally convenient for travel at every part of its width, and still have enough lateral slope to cause water to run off from it.

It is especially desirable that no surface-water flowing from the road-side (above all, when frost is coming out of the ground in the Spring) be permitted to run on to the road. This should be effectively prevented by the formation of sufficient gutters, with such outlets as will prevent ponding at the sides of the road. When it is necessary to carry the water of the gutters from one side of the road to the other, culverts should be provided; and wherever the slope of the road is sufficient to cause water to flow along it lengthwise—that is, wherever the inclination is more than about one in fifty—there should be frequent slight depressions *from the center diagonally toward the gutters* to carry the flow away before it can accumulate sufficiently to form a washing current.

If it can be done without hauling additional material, it is always well to raise the road-bed somewhat above the level of the adjoining land, and this may usually be accomplished by throwing upon it the subsoil of the gutters. *In no case should surface-soil, sods, or fine road-mud be used for repairs. The most serious objection to the absurd system of road mending so common in this country lies in the fact that the annual repairing is little more than the ploughing up and throwing back upon the roadway of the soft and unsuitable material which has been washed into the gutters.*

It is easy, in the country, to have the grades of all roadways so regulated as to shed rain-water falling upon them, and to have them so furnished with side gutters as to prevent water from the road-side from running on to them. The simplest way to effect this, and the neatest way, too, is to make gutters outside of the line of the road, say six inches deep and eight feet wide, these being at once sodded or sown with grass and grain to give an early protection against washing; made on such a shallow curve, they will afford no obstruction to any system of mowing that may be adopted, while their great width will give them sufficient capacity to carry away the water of considerable storms.

The work of construction having been duly attended to, it is no less important to provide for regular and constant care. Any rutting that comes of heavy traffic in bad weather should be obliterated either by raking, or, better still, by filling the ruts with gravel or ashes. *If such work is attended to immediately on the occasion for it arising, the amount of labor required will be very slight; for it is especially true with reference to roads, that "a stitch in time saves nine."* If the filling of ruts and wheel-tracks be done in time, the serious damage that comes from guttering flows of water lengthwise along the road may be almost entirely avoided. —[*Extracts, with permission, from Waring's "Village Improvements and Farm Villages," published by Houghton, Mifflin & Co., Boston, Mass. See, also, Gillespie's Roads and Railroads.*

Lawns—Best Mixtures of Grass Seeds.

Charles L. Flint, in his book entitled "Grasses and Forage Plants," recommends the following mixtures:

He says: "If the object be to make a permanent lawn, as is frequently desirable, around or in sight of the farm-house, something like the following mixture will generally be found to give satisfactory results:

	POUNDS.
Meadow Foxtail	2
Sweet-scented Vernal Grasses	1
Redtop	2
Hard Fescue	3
Sheep's Fescue	1
Meadow Fescue	4
Red Fescue	2
Italian Rye Grass	3
Perennial Rye Grass	6
Timothy	3
June Grass	4
Rough-stalked Meadow Grass	2
Yellow Oat Grass	1
Perennial Clover	2
Red Clover	2
White Clover	6
Total	44

This mixture will resist the effects of our severe droughts better than those commonly used for lawns. If anything is omitted from it, the red and perennial clovers, the yellow oat grass, and a part of the rye grass could best be spared. Red clover, like other coarse and large-leaved plants, rather mars the beauty of fine lawns; though, as it disappears mostly after the second year, it may be of service in protecting the finer grasses. Lawns kept frequently mown are of most use as furnishing food for calves and sheep, and are less adapted to supply the wants of larger animals.

Another mixture for lawns and pleasure grounds, which are to be often mown or kept short, is recommended by Parnell, as follows:

	POUNDS.
Crested Dog's-tail	11
Yellow Oat Grass	8
Hard Fescue	5
Wood Meadow	4
June Grass	2
Rough-stalked Meadow	2
Redtop	4
Whitetop	4
Total	40

Lawns furnished with suitable grasses become much finer and more velvety, from frequent mowing, than they otherwise would be. The Lawson's mixture, for lawns frequently mown, consists mainly of the same species, but in different proportions. It is as follows:

	POUNDS.
Crested Dog's-tail	10
Hard Fescue	4
Slender Fescue	2
Perennial Rye Grass	10
Wood Meadow Grass	2
Rough-stalked Meadow	1
Yellow Oat Grass	1
June Grass	8
White Clover	8
Total	46

A mixture for permanent lawn pastures, or pastures lying in the vicinity of dwellings or public highways, where the owner has some regard to fineness and beauty of herbage, should, I think, be composed of a still larger number of species.

The following is suggested as most likely to secure the end desired:

	POUNDS.
Meadow Foxtail	3
Sweet-scented Vernal	2
Orchard Grass	3
Hard Fescue	2
Sheep's Fescue	2
Meadow Fescue	2

	POUNDS.
Italian Rye Grass	3
Perennial Rye Grass	4
Timothy	3
Redtop	3
June Grass	4
Rough-stalked Meadow	3
Yellow Oat Grass	1
Red Clover	2
Perennial Red Clover	2
White Clover	4
Total	43

In all such mixtures the early Spring and the late Autumn growth, as well as the general luxuriance of the Summer herbage, are to be regarded. Grasses, therefore, which are characterized by their early and late growth, become of great value and importance in the mixture, even though their nutritive qualities are slight, and though they may be comparatively valueless as field grasses to be mown for hay."

Factory Adornment.

An important work of rural improvement in many towns, would be the betterment of the surroundings of their factories. Too frequently these grounds are disfigured with rubbish, and made unsightly by neglect. Keep a man in a pig-sty, and he would become swinish in his habits, but reverse these conditions, and you reverse the results. The influence of flowers, shrubbery, or neat and cultivated grounds, upon operatives, in refining their taste and promoting their happiness, I contend is too often ignored. There is, however, a goodly number of our most successful manufacturers, who show their interest in their hands by making their factory buildings and tenement-houses inviting, comfortable and healthful, and adorning the surrounding grounds.

The two model manufacturing villages of America, and, so far as I have been able to observe, of the world—the Cheney Silk Factory, in South Manchester, Connecticut, and the Fairbanks Scale Works, in St. Johnsbury, Vermont—happily illustrate the desirableness and results of better provisions for the taste and comfort of operatives. I do not assume that all factories can fully adopt the high standard of these remarkable establishments, which are exceptional in their opportunities. There are serious embarrassments in large manufacturing towns, especially where the factories are controlled by non-resident owners, more anxious for dividends than for the comfort and improvement of their workmen.

In the factories above named, there has evidently been mutual sympathy and interest between employers and employed. The senior Governor Fairbanks used to say to his men, "You should always come to me as to a father." He maintained relations of kindness with them, visiting the sick, helping the needy, counseling the erring, encouraging their thrift and enjoining habits of economy. He taught them that it was their interest and duty "to lay up something every month." He was a conspicuous example at once of strict economy and princely liberality. The fact that so many of the workmen here are "forehanded," besides owning their homesteads, is due to his teaching and example. The worth and dignity of work he illustrated in theory and practice. His sons worked in the shop and thoroughly learned the trade. Of course there is here the happiest conciliation between labor and capital. It is not strange that the workmen "hold on." Many have worked in this factory from twenty to forty years. The liberal provisions for the education, improvement, happiness and prosperity of the hands, explain the absence of discontent, and the uniform good feeling and harmony which prevail. How to harmonize labor and capital, is now one of the great questions of the age. Many millions of money have been lately lost in this country and in England, by needless antagonisms between those who should be partners.

B. G. NORTHROP.

The Lenox System of Sewage, as described by Col. Waring, in his "Village Improvements."

"The third system—the distribution of sewage through irrigation pipes laid at the depth of ten or twelve inches below the surface of the ground—has its efficiency attested by numerous instances in private grounds. I have adopted this system for disposing of the sewage of the village of Lenox, Mass., where there was no other means available short of cutting an outlet, at great expense, through a considerable elevation. This method is an extremely simple one, and is available in every instance where even a small area of land lying slightly below the level of the outlet is to be commanded. The arrangement of the sub-irrigation pipes is easily made: Suppose that in land having an inclination of about one in two hundred, occupied by grass or other growth, a trench be dug twelve inches deep, that there be laid upon the bottom of this trench a narrow strip of plank to insure a uniform grade, and that upon this plank is laid a line of common agricultural land-drain tiles, say two inches in diameter. However carefully these tiles may be placed, there will be at their joints a sufficient space for the leaking out of any liquid they may contain; the tiles being laid either with collars around the joints, or with bits of paper laid over them, to prevent the rattling in of loose earth during the filling. The excavated earth is to be returned to its place, well compacted, and covered with its sod. Suppose this drain to have a cross-section equal to three square inches, and a length of one hundred feet, its capacity will equal about sixteen gallons, or a half-barrel. If this amount of liquid be rapidly discharged into the drain, the inclination being slight, it will at once be filled or nearly filled for its whole length, and the liquid will leak away in tolerably uniform proportion at every joint along the line, and will saturate the surrounding earth. The plan adopted at Lenox, and recommended for all small villages which cannot secure a better outlet, is simply a multiplication of these drains to a sufficient extent.

A description of the manner in which the Lenox work is arranged will illustrate the adaptation of the system to its circumstances. As circumstances vary, the adaptation must be modified. (See Diagram.)

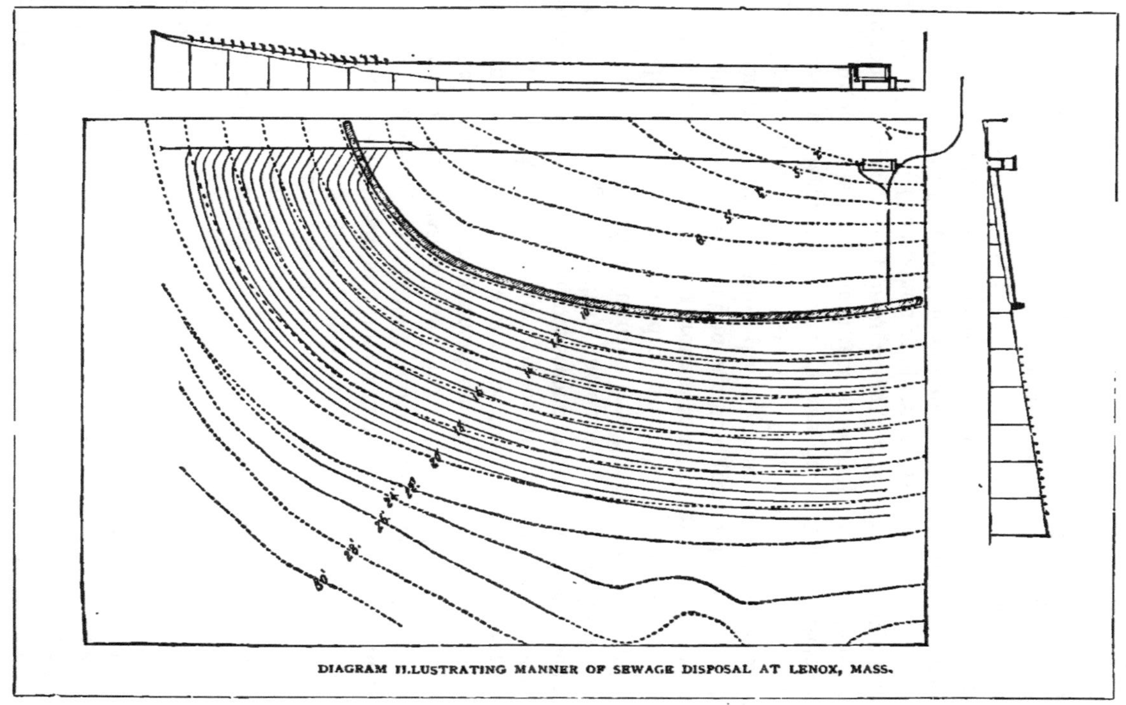

DIAGRAM ILLUSTRATING MANNER OF SEWAGE DISPOSAL AT LENOX, MASS.

The main outlet sewer delivers at a distance of about one-half mile from the last junction with a branch sewer. It is a six-inch pipe five feet below the surface of the ground, and it delivers into a flush-tank like that shown on page 51, but having a capacity of about five hundred cubic feet. This tank stands at the upper side of a field having an inclination of seven in one hundred. There is a branch from the main sewer, above the tank, supplied with a stop-cock, by which, in case of need, the sewage may be carried on down the hill without going into the tank. The outlet from the chamber below the siphon leads off in another direction down the hill, and has a stop-cock and a branch which will allow its flow to be diverted. The discharge of this diverted stream and the discharge through the branch of the main above the tank, both deliver into a horizontal surface gutter to be well grassed, and lying at the top of the land to be irrigated. By this arrangement, should repairs become necessary in the tank, the flow may be turned into the gutter; or, should it be desired for any reason to use the outflow of the tank for surface irrigation, the second branch outlet will deliver it into the same gutter, where, the outflow being uniform along the whole length of five hundred feet, the stream will pass in a thin sheet off on the descending ground. The hill-side immediately below the gutter, is brought to a true grade and covered with grass. As its inclination is much greater than would be admissible for sub-irrigation drains, these are laid *obliquely* in parallel lines at intervals of six feet from one end to the other over the whole graded slope. These drains are connected at their upper ends with the direct outlet-pipe leading from the siphon chamber. They have an aggregate length of about ten thousand feet. The method of operation is as follows:

The capacity of the tank is supposed to equal about two days' discharge, or about thirty-five hundred gallons; and the whole capacity of the drains is about half that of the tank, so that the rapid emptying of the whole volume into them will insure their being pretty thoroughly filled from end to end. This arrangement will provide for the saturation of the soil about once in two days, and will leave a sufficient interval between the periods of saturation for the thorough dispersal and aeration of the filth.

The extent to which this system will be interfered with by frost, it is impossible to say. This will probably be less than would be supposed, for the reason that the ground would often be covered with snow, and that the sewage will have sufficient warmth to exert considerable thawing influence. Whenever the discharge of the liquid through irrigation pipes is shown to have become obstructed by freezing, it will only be necessary to divert the flow, and turn it into the surface gutter to be distributed over the ground.

It is possible that in this case, as in the one which has been under my observation for six years past, there will be no interruption of the working because of cold; but, should the interruption become serious, I shall propose the planting of evergreen trees in parallel rows midway between the drains. The protection that would thus be afforded, both by the trees and by the drifting snow which they would gather, would probably keep the ground free throughout the Winter. Incidentally to the chief advantage of this system, there will be, so long as the land is in grass, quite an addition to its product."

For further information, see Col. Waring's Report, in the preceding pages.

Drainage for Health.

Col. Waring discusses fully the subject of the disposal of house wastes and protection of wells. The object of this note is to impress a not less important point, viz., the duty of securing such subsoil drainage as will insure dryness of the site of foundation walls and of the cellar.

Lord Bacon has said: " He who builds a fair house upon an ill seat, committeth himself to prison."

As a rule, the dry soils, sand and gravel, are the healthiest. Coarse gravel is also the safest soil to build upon, as it is almost incompressible and makes a firm foundation.

While typhoid fever and diphtheria are conceded to be generated and their virulence increased by impure air and water, two other prevalent scourges, *consumption* and *fever and ague*, are caused by the influence of stagnant water and excessive wetness of the soil; and they may be much alleviated by the simple removal of the drainage water, through exactly the same process that is employed in farm drainage.

We will consider first the mode to be adopted to secure

DRYNESS OF SITE.

As our space is limited, we must ask the reader to be content, on many points, with simple rules and directions, without discussion of reasons.

To drain a tract, large or small, find an outlet low enough to give the necessary fall—one foot in one hundred is sufficient, and drains will work well with but one-quarter of that fall. If the fall is slight, the greater care will be necessary in laying out and performing the work.

The work should be all laid out before breaking ground. Usually a single main drain should run through the lowest part of the tract, and it is not important that the main should be straight as to line, but there must be no inequality in the grade. Having laid out the main, lay side drains running into it, having in view two principles: First, to run each drain up and down the slope of the land, rather than across; and, second, to have them parallel to each other. Like most principles, we shall be compelled often to compromise them. The depth should be four feet or more, and the distance apart, with this depth, may be from thirty to fifty feet.

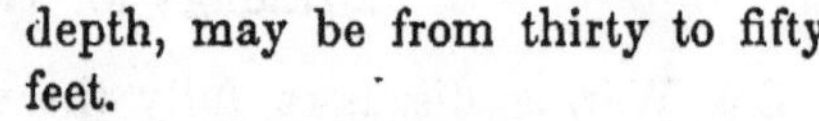

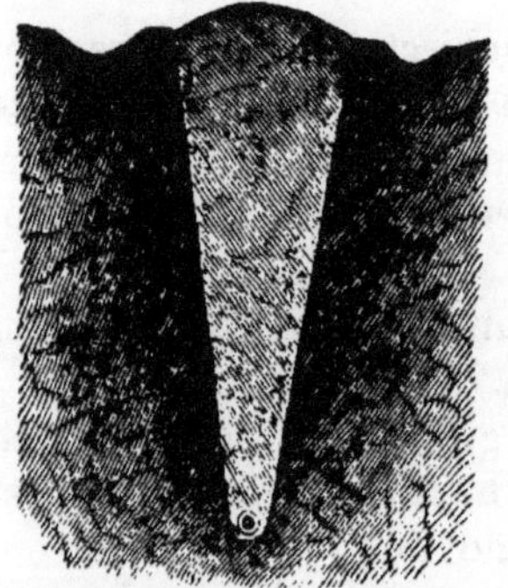

FIG. 1.—PROPER SHAPE FOR A TRENCH.

To open them, begin at the outlet, so that the water may run off as the work proceeds, and with a common spade and pick, cut a trench by a line, eighteen inches wide at the surface, narrowing to four inches, or the width of a laborer's boot, at the bottom. To finish the bottom, a spade four inches wide is necessary, and may be made by getting a blacksmith to cut down a common long-handled shovel to that width, no wider at the heel than the point. Common drain tiles are recommended, and the directions given are specially adapted to their use.

The drains being thus opened, we begin to lay the tiles at the upper end. Lay the first tile (usually of two-inch size) with a brick or flat stone over the upper end, to close it entirely, and the next end to end with it, and so on to the main, keeping always an inclination, however slight, for if any depression is made, the silt will lodge in it and obstruct the work.

Here let this idea be fully impressed: In this system of drainage no water is to be anywhere admitted except by percolation through the soil. There is to be no opening to the surface, or into any ditch, or to receive sink-water, or anything but clear water creeping underground.

But how does the water get in? Chiefly at the joints, which are as close as two rough bricks laid end to end would be. Nothing short of cementing the joints can keep the water out. The great difficulty is to keep out silt or fine sand.

Having laid two or three tiles on the bare earth, if hard (and on pieces of laths or other thin wood, if soft), cover each joint half or more round the tiles with a piece of tarred paper as large as a common letter envelope, and, holding the whole firmly, place soil or gravel over it and on both sides of the tiles, pressing it enough to keep them in place. However tempted to do so, put no stones nor straw nor shavings into the drain. Cover and fill up with anything at hand except soft clay, fine sand or sods, which should not be placed in contact with the tiles.

When we approach the junction of the minor drain with the main, a curve should be made, so as not to bring in the side stream at right angles. Branch tiles may be found made for the purpose of junction, and these are much better than any home contrivances. The last few feet of the main should be of vitrified pipe, with cemented joints.

Having thus connected the drains in one system with only one outlet, this should be so secured by a wire grating that no frog or other creeping thing can explore it, and it should be built up solid with stone, so as to be permanent, and should have a clean fall of a few inches upon a flat stone, that it may not be obstructed by back-water and mud.

The above instructions, if followed, will insure a dry site, but in the case of particularly springy ground, or where a house is situated on a side hill, it may be well to drain the cellar itself.

This may be done by digging a trench as above directed, in the cellar, as close to the wall as it can safely be dug, and to a depth six inches below the bottom of the foundation. The bottom of this trench should have a slight but regular fall toward the point where the pipe can most conveniently be carried under the foundation to an outlet built as above directed, and

FIG. 2.—OUTLET.

the last few feet will be best constructed of vitrified pipe, with tightly cemented joints, in order to make a lasting job.

Under no circumstances should these pipes be connected with the sewer pipes or cesspools.

By this simple method damp walls and cellars may be entirely cured at a small expense for material and about a day's labor of a couple of careful men.

The directions given above for laying the pipes and filling the trench should be exactly followed.

It has been scientifically demonstrated that damp sites, and particularly damp cellars aggravate and to a large extent produce consumption and malarial disorders. It is a fact that where the drainage of building sites and of cellars has been attended to, deaths from consumption have fallen off fifty per cent.

Which are of *greater value*, the few dollars it will cost to make our homes healthy, or the life and health of our wives and little ones?

Which will *cost less*, to spend a few dollars in prevention, or many dollars in the cure or attempt to cure disease?

[*Condensed from the Fourth Annual Report of the State Board of Health of Massachusetts.*

Filtering Cisterns.

As there may be some of our members who propose constructing cisterns for retaining their supply of drinking water, the following description and illustration from "The Sanitary Engineer" for November 1st, 1880, are given:

"The best material for rain water cisterns is brick, laid in hydraulic cement and plastered inside. No lime should be used for the plastering, but a mortar made of equal parts of cement and good, clean, sharp sand. This is rarely found clean enough to be used without first washing it. After the plastering is hard, it should be washed twice with a grout of cement and water, without sand, applied with a white-wash brush. If the ground is firm, and stands plumb without caving in, one layer of brick laid directly against the side of the pit is enough. In this case the form of the pit should be carefully trimmed to a true circle, and the walls trimmed plumb. Then the brick work can be laid directly against it, filling all small cavities between the brick and ground with cement, and not with earth. If the ground is not firm enough to stand in this way, a thicker wall will be needed, say eight inches. The earth that is filled around it should be puddled in with plenty of water, to ensure a solid packing. Ramming the earth without puddling is not so good, and will not be likely to prevent the cistern from bursting when first filled with water. A very small crack will spoil it. The floor can be laid after the walls are plastered, so as to avoid stepping on it much after laying it. The floor should be dished like a saucer, to facilitate cleaning out.

"For filtering, build a partition in the cistern by which any portion, say one-fourth, of its contents can be separated from the remainder. Insert the suction pipe or pump within this chamber, and allow the inlets to discharge outside of it in the larger part of the cistern. If the partition is built of one thick-

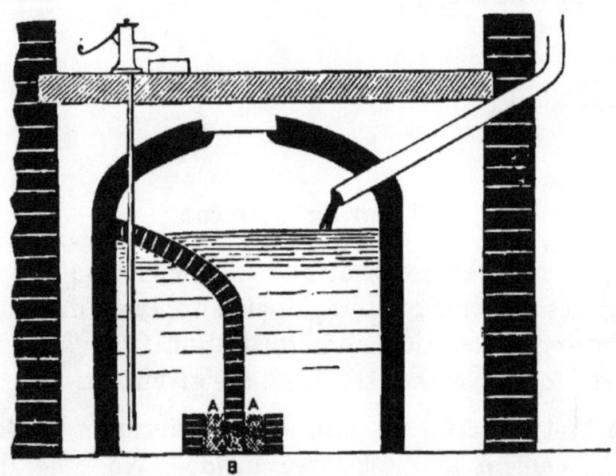

ness of soft, porous brick, the water will soak through it; but this brick partition should be domed over against the side walls to prevent any pollution of the filtered water by dust or spatterings from above. If the water is quite foul, the pores of the bricks will be choked in time, and refuse to pass more water. In that case the partition must be renewed, or holes made near the bottom, in which sponges, broken charcoal or sand can be placed to do the work; and these can be renewed when found necessary.

"If gravel and charcoal are used, they are deposited in layers, charcoal at bottom, and a few inches of gravel on top, each side the filtering wall at *A A* [see cut], and confined by dwarf walls on each side. Holes are left in the base of the filtering wall by omitting alternate bricks in the bottom course. The water is then filtered by passing down through one bed of charcoal and up through the other. The gravel is chiefly useful to put on top of the charcoal to protect it from wash.

"This charcoal will need frequent renewal if there is much solid matter in the water. Hence two cisterns are convenient."

Two other illustrations are given, showing a somewhat different construction. These are taken from "Wood's Household

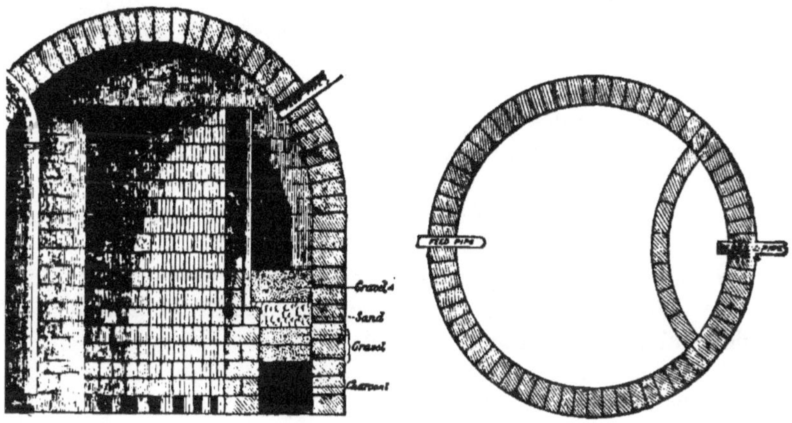

Practice," a valuable work on hygiene. They explain themselves sufficiently without need of description.

Heating and Ventilation.

The object of this note is to explain in a simple way how we may keep our houses comfortably warm in Winter, and yet not compel ourselves to breathe over and over again air which has become dirty and foul from washing out our lungs and contact with our bodies.

Col. Waring has entered a plea for "a pure soil" and "pure water;" now, pray heed Hippocrates once more, and be sure you have an ample supply of pure, life-giving air in your dwellings.

Dr. Hamilton Osgood, in his admirable little book on "Winter and its Dangers," says: "Human beings, as well as fish, live, move and have their being in a fluid. That in which we find fish is visible, and its slightest impurity noticeable. Not so the fluid in which we live. It is invisible, and, in a general sense, so are its impurities. Eyes being of no use here, the sense of smell, if properly regarded, will be our protector. When the air of our rooms is foul, when drains are imperfect, when any impure thing taints the atmosphere, the sense of smell gives us warnings which should be religiously regarded and never neglected.

"The air in which we live, and which we inhale, is composed, when normally pure, of eighty parts nitrogen, about twenty parts of oxygen, and a small quantity of carbonic acid, say about four-hundredths of one per cent. When absolutely pure, the air, of course, is absolutely free from this poisonous element. Our health depends upon keeping up the twenty per cent. of oxygen and keeping down the carbonic acid to its lowest possible minimum. An increase of this gas to five or ten per cent. would be fatal to life.

"When the blood leaves the lungs, it is in the condition called arterial—that is, it has been purified by the air, or aerified. And the name artery originated in the fact that, until the time of Galen, in the second century of our era, the blood-vessels leading from the lungs and heart were supposed to convey air directly from the windpipe, and air only, because after death they are always found empty. It was thought that the veins, the vessels which bring the blood back to the heart and lungs, were the only channels of the blood, for after death they were always found full.

"The blood carries myriads of small bodies, called blood-corpuscles, which, with the exception of a few white ones, existing in the proportion of about four to one thousand of the red, have a color which is bright red when the blood is pure or arterial, purplish or dark crimson when the blood is impure or venus. These bodies have aptly been compared to boats. When the blood leaves the lungs, these boats carry a mixed cargo, an important portion of which is oxygen. This they discharge as they pass through the canals of the body, some stopping here, some there; but they always exchange it for an equal load of carbonic acid. This carbonic acid changes the color of these dainty boats from dark to bright red. When they reach the lungs again, they expect to find a new cargo of oxygen, and likewise to become purified and restored to their original brightness. Consequently, when the air inhaled by the lungs is once in the air-cells, which cluster about the finer bronchial tubes like grapes upon their stems, the pure air finds a quantity of carbonic acid which has been brought by the boats that have just arrived from the rivers and canals of the body.

"By a wonderful process of which gases are capable, the carbonic acid from the boats and the oxygen from the inspired air both pass through two exquisitely delicate walls which separate the blood in the vessels from the air in the air-cells of the lungs, and exchange places—the air in the lungs take the carbonic acid from the impure blood, and becoming itself impure; the blood-corpuscles, or the boats, taking the oxygen from the pure air *(if only it be pure)*, and thus becoming purified. Where this latter takes place, the air-cells lie in a perfect mesh of the most delicate vessels conceivable. The walls of each are so exceedingly thin that the transfusion or passage through them of the two gases is made possible. But for this delicacy of construction, the exchange could not take place. The freshly-laden boats now start on a new trip, their places being instantly taken by others. The impure air is exhaled, and the new inspiration sends fresh air to the air-cells and the waiting boats. And so this wonderful process of exchange goes on day and night, whether we are sleeping or waking."

"It is undoubted," says the same author, "that affections of the lungs, notably consumption, find their origin in inhaled air which is laden with organic vapors and particles arising from the human body." He also attributes bronchial affections, "colds," lassitude, head-aches and general dibility largely to the breathing of impure air.

"Think, too," he continues "of the air of church, theater and crowded parlor. Go into such from the fresh air an hour after the company has assembled. How heavy the air with personal effluvia and rebreathed breath. Pah! these delicate women have no thought of what they are doing. Offer such an one a cup of ditch water; would she drink it? Would she drink it if it contained even a speck? No. And yet think of it: in unventilated rooms and crowded assemblies, we inhale dirty air—air which has washed out other lungs than ours, some of them probably in a state of disease! Such air contains personal impurities, particles from the lungs, uncleanly odors. Such air drawn into sensitive lungs—lungs which are only waiting to spring into inflamed conditions—creates disease." * * * * "God gives us pure air. Is it not a sin and a shame that we do not keep it pure? Think, too, of the sick, of the delicate, of the children who are confined to the house. They are mainly helpless. For their pure air they are dependent upon the foresight of others, and it is just as cruel to keep it from them as it would be to deny them food, and almost as dangerous. *Their lives depend upon it. They die for want of it.*"

One other quotation, and then we are done: "It is a very common belief that night air is unhealthful; but, as Florence Nightingale sensibly remarks, 'we must breathe night air at night;' and she might have added: if pure night air is shut out, then we breathe foul night air." * * * * "Statistics show that where war has slain its thousands, bad night air has slain its tens of thousands; then do not fear, but welcome the pure air of night."

"Better is it," says a wise writer, "to spend money on a supply of pure air than on carven work and orations."

How to obtain this supply of pure air in the Winter months, without producing draughts and without causing an undue waste of fuel, I now propose to state in a few plain words. Those who desire to study the subject more fully, I refer to the series of articles on the subject in "The Sanitary Engineer," by Dr. John S. Billings, U. S. A.

Most country-houses—and to those, these remarks are intended more particularly to apply—are provided with ample fire-places. Let the first step taken be to open these, substituting for the tight fire-board either such screens as are used in windows in the Summer time; or, better yet, let the andirons be polished and placed on the hearth as in "ye olden time." You now have provided a means of escape for the foul air which is constantly entering the room from lungs and lamps and emanations from your bodies.

Now, it is necessary to replace this bad air which you have sent up the chimney, with "good, pure country air." This may be done, of course, by opening windows or doors, but we all know that in the cold Winter time this would be, to say the least, very uncomfortable. The cheapest and simplest way to introduce pure air without causing draughts, is to provide several strips of wood one-third of an inch thick, of various widths, from two to six inches, and long enough to fit the window-frame under the lower sash. The latter is then raised, and the strip inserted under it, thus closing the aperture. There will, in this way, be left between the upper and lower sash a space where air can enter, which may vary in size with the weather, according to the thickness of the strip used. The air coming through this space is deflected toward the ceiling by the lower sash, and thus enters the room without any danger of causing a draught or otherwise annoying the occupants. [Fig. 1.]

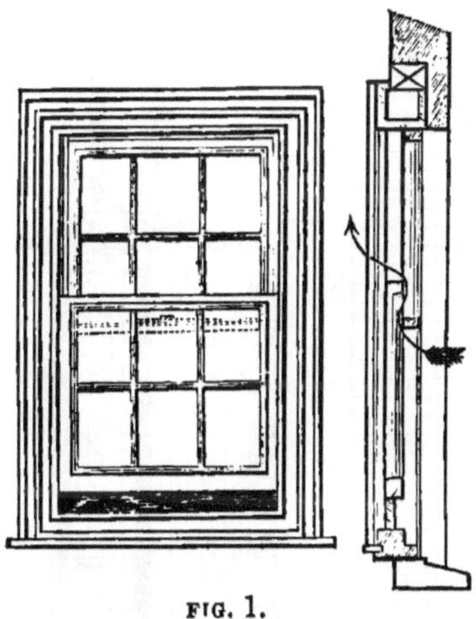

FIG. 1.

The method just described will be useful at all seasons, when it is necessary to keep windows and doors closed, especially in stormy weather in Spring, Summer and Fall, and in the cool, Fall evenings before the fire is started.

The following suggestions from an article by Rev. Daniel C. Jacokes, in "Carpentry and Building," for November, 1880, are admirably adapted for houses mostly heated by stoves and not provided with open fire-places:

"During cold weather, ventilation should be produced by the aid of heat. The following rules should be carefully observed in heating and ventilating:

"1. Conduct, in some convenient manner, out-door air against a heated surface.

"2. Conduct the in-door air from the floor into a heated flue. In this manner a complete circulation of air may be had, and an abundant supply of pure warm air may be secured; pro-

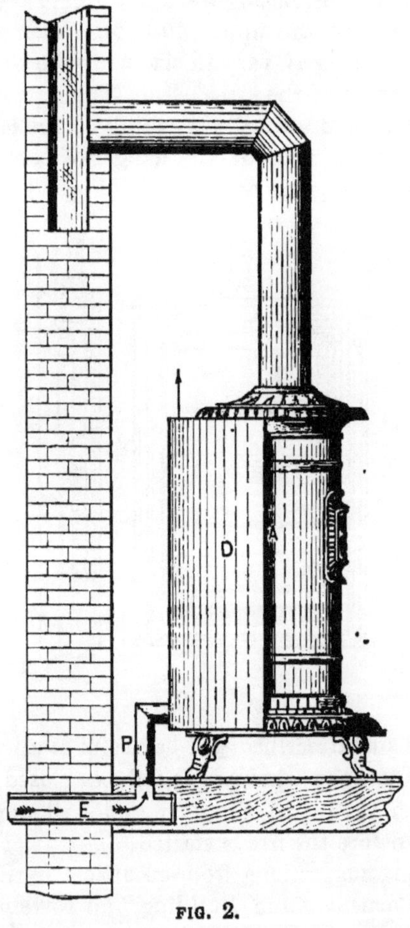

FIG. 2.

vided, first, that the ducts be sufficiently large; and, second, that the dust in the air be not burned by a red-hot surface. If these rules are observed, the heating and ventilating will be very economical and satisfactory. Most of the buildings, public and private, for human use are constructed without any reference to ventilation; indeed, most of them seem to have been planned to prevent the possibility of either the light of the sun or the pure air of heaven entering them. There is, consequently, much difficulty in properly heating or ventilating them. Those who prefer health to the sight of the changes necessary in each case to secure such an end, must not object to see an additional pipe to convey foul air out of the room, and, also, a pipe to convey the pure outdoor air into it.

"There are many buildings heated by a furnace. In these the pure outdoor air is properly heated; but where there is no preparation for ventilation, this may be secured in the same manner as when heated by a stove.

"The great majority of houses are heated by stoves. The outdoor air in such cases must be conducted to the surface of the stove, as illustrated by the following diagrams. These stoves have various shapes; whatever they may be, the principles will here be explained, so that any person may modify the method so as to secure the result desired. Fig. 2 shows how a sheet-iron jacket may be fitted to the back of a stove for heating the outdoor air brought within the jacket against the stove. The jacket is seen at the top of the stove, and is represented by the line marked D. The jacket should never be more than 4½ inches from the back of the stove, and should always be closed at the bottom, so that the air in the room will never be reheated and breathed over and over again. This should be remembered. whatever kind or form of jacket is used.

"Fig. 3 illustrates the manner of conducting the outdoor air to the stove within the jacket for heating.

"A wood stove may be jacketed in the same manner as a coal stove. In this case the jacket may be fitted to the sides of the stove very nicely, covering the back of the stove in the same manner as the coal stove, so that the sheet-iron jacket will be at an average distance of 4½ inches from the back; never more than this.

"Outdoor air may also be heated by conducting it within a jacket around the stove-pipe of a wood or coal stove, as shown in section in Fig. 4.

"In school-houses, where box stoves are mostly used, a sheet-iron jacket may inclose the stove excepting the front, which should be left open for the escape of the heated air. The space between the stove and jacket should be 4 inches—not more—on the sides and top; on the back the jacket may be as wide as the hole in the floor—6 inches. An opening should be made through the floor at the back end of the stove near the jacket, 6 by 16 inches, if the jacket is wide enough to cover it. A pipe,

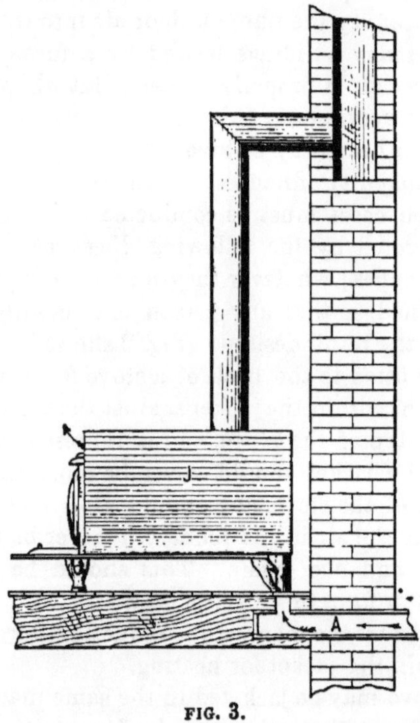

FIG. 3.

the shape of the hole, should be fitted so as to reach a little above the bottom of the stove, that the air may reach the heated surface at once. Fig. 3 snows this arrangement.

"Ventilation, according to rule second, should always convey the indoor air from the floor into a heated flue. If the chimney is properly constructed, this may be done with little expense or trouble. Usually, however, this is not the case. The general rule is to build chimneys very small—mostly 4 by 12 or 16 inches on the inside. This narrow space will soon be more or less filled with soot. In such cases ventilation will be difficult, if not impossible. If the chimney has been constructed with an apartment for ventilation, it will be sufficient to make an opening into it at the floor—that is, the bottom of the opening

FIG. 4.

must in all cases be exactly even with the top of the floor, otherwise the ventilation will be imperfect; this will give good ventilation. All chimneys should be constructed with an apartment for each story, as shown in Fig. 5, and should be plastered smooth; the partition should be made of brick, and built single width, so that it will be four inches thick. This wall will be constantly heated to keep a continual draft in the ventilating flue.

"If a chimney is sufficiently large, a 7 or 8-inch stove-pipe—or larger, if possible—may be let down inside of the chimney and turned into the room at the floor by an elbow; this will make an efficient ventilator. If there is not sufficient room, or if for any other cause, as a crooked chimney, this cannot be done, ventilation may be effected as illustrated in Fig. 6. Take a pipe one inch smaller in diameter than the supply pipe which is to conduct the outdoor air to the stove, and carry it into the chimney—if possible, below the entrance of the smoke-pipe. This plan can be adopted more frequently and at less cost than any other, as chimneys are generally constructed.

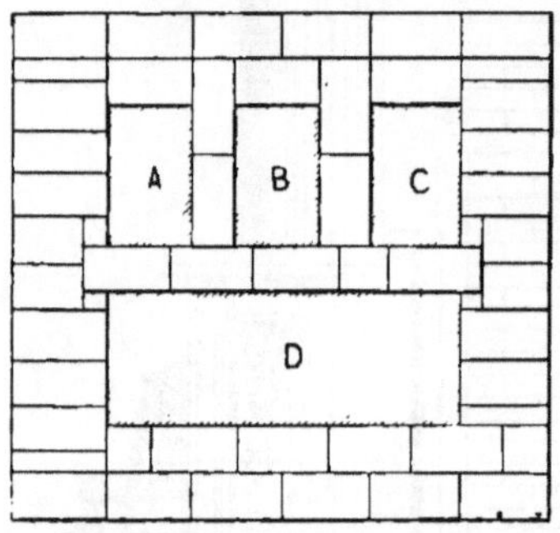

FIG. 5.—CONSTRUCTION OF CHIMNEY FOR BOTH SMOKE AND VENTILATION. D, SMOKE FLUE. A, VENTILATION FLUE FOR FIRST STORY. B, VENTILATION FLUE FOR SECOND STORY. C, VENTILATION FLUE FOR THIRD STORY.

"In many houses the chimney is so constructed or situated that the ventilation would not be equal to the work required. Such an instance would be when the chimney is short, the bottom being near the ceiling in the upper story, with a stove in each story connected with it. In such cases ventilation would be hardly possible. To remedy this the following plan may be adopted: The stove-pipe in the second story may be surrounded by a much larger pipe; a 6-inch pipe may be surrounded by a 10-inch pipe; a 7-inch by a 12-inch jacket pipe, and the ventilator may be connected with this surrounding jacket. The stove-pipe and the jacket are both to be carried into the chimney as one pipe; the stove-pipe within will so heat the surrounding air that a strong ventilation will be the result. The ventilator should enter the jacket at or near its bottom, as seen in Fig. 7.

"This plan, as well as the others recommended, will secure good heating and ventilation at a very moderate cost. I have

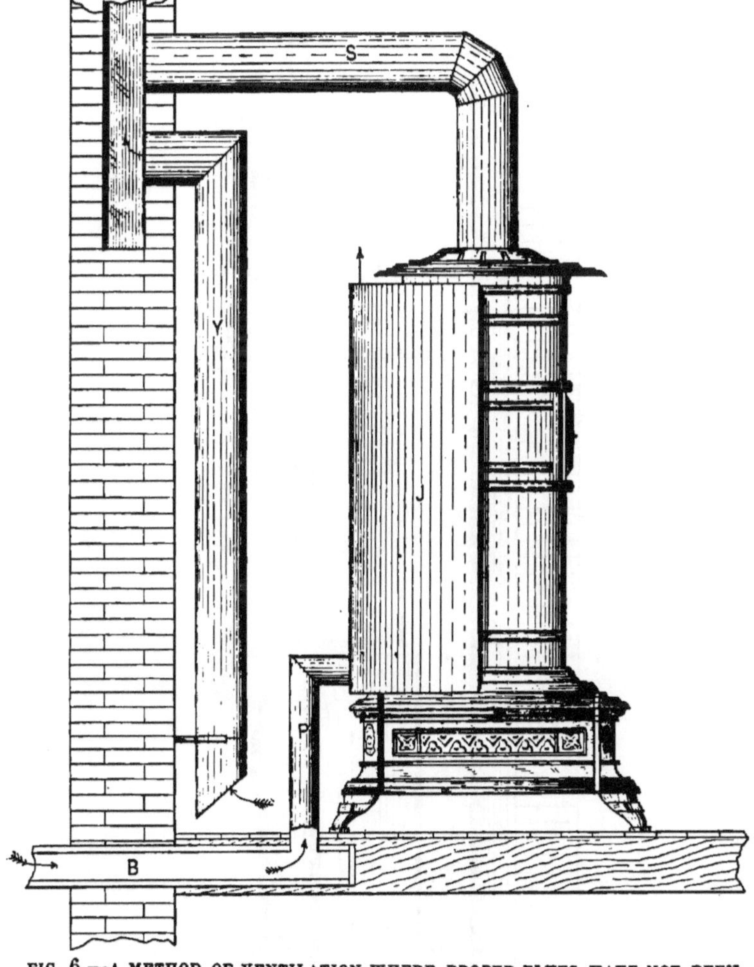

FIG. 6.—A METHOD OF VENTILATION WHERE PROPER FLUES HAVE NOT BEEN PROVIDED. S, STOVE PIPE. V, VENTILATOR PIPE, 6 INCHES DIAMETER, AND OPEN NEAR FLOOR. B, SUPPLY OF OUTDOOR AIR. P, SUPPLY PIPE (OVAL IN SECTIONS). J, JACKET OF STOVE.

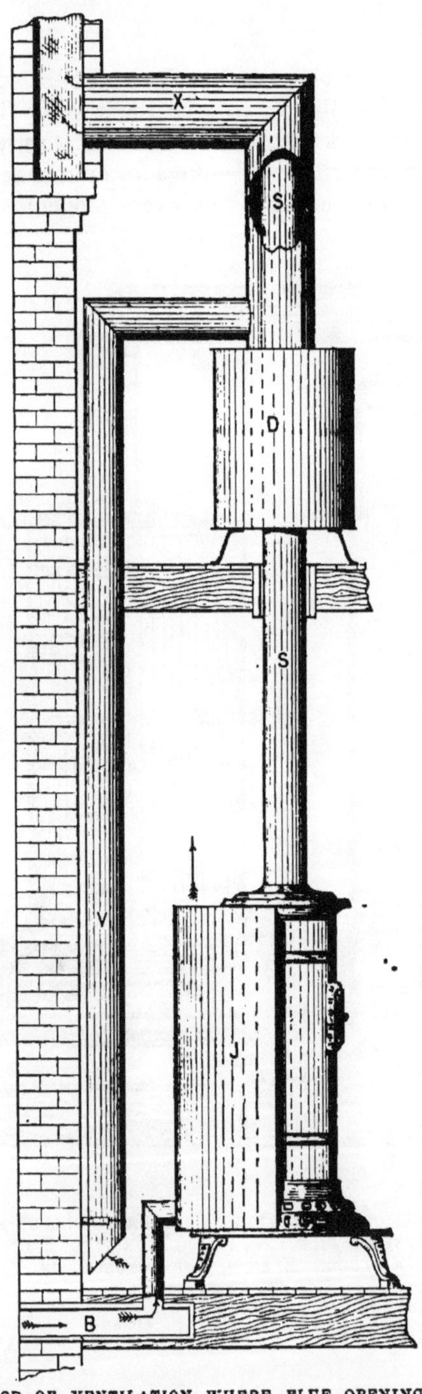

FIG. 7.—METHOD OF VENTILATION WHERE FLUE OPENING IS IN SECOND STORY. B, SUPPLY OF OUTSIDE AIR. V, VENTILATING PIPE. S, STOVE PIPE. J, JACKET TO STOVE. D, DRUM, LOCATED IN SECOND STORY. X, JACKET TO STOVE-PIPE, BY WHICH THE AIR WITHDRAWN FROM LOWER ROOM IS SOMEWHAT HEATED BEFORE ENTERING CHIMNEY FLUE.

known it to cost from ten shillings in the simpler forms to ten dollars by the more complicated forms; so that healthy and comfortable homes may be enjoyed by the poor as well as by the more favored of our fellow-citizens.

"The ventilation of churches, schools and other public buildings where large numbers of persons assemble, is of the highest importance. The general practice is to construct very small chimneys, which renders it difficult to secure efficient ventilation. In all these cases it would be better to reconstruct them, making them, say, 16 by 36 inches inside, dividing the space into two or more apartments, if there is one story to be warmed, or into three if two stories—one for the smoke, the others for ventilation—with an opening into each ventilating flue, always at the floor. One church has a chimney 16 by 36 inches inside, divided by putting a 16-inch pipe of heavy sheet iron so as to make the side flues of equal size; the pipe is fitted close to the brick wall to secure it to its place. This is the smoke-pipe, and it warms the air almost instantly in the foul-air flues at its sides, making a very powerful ventilator. This church has a basement story, and needs two flues, one for each room. If this pipe should ever be destroyed, another can be slipped inside of it and thus renewed. In public buildings which are heated at intervals this sheet-iron pipe is the best, as it heats the air on each side at once. In a building constantly heated the best way would be to build the partitions in the chimney with brick. The flues should always be plastered smooth. When this cannot be done, the ventilation must be made in the same manner as for dwelling-houses, the ventilating pipes being correspondingly large.

"In another church a jacket pipe 16 inches in diameter was put around a stove-pipe 7 inches in diameter, connected with a stove—all in the room below—and carried into the chimney. The end of the jacket opposite to the chimney was turned up through the floor by an elbow to receive the foul air of the room above and discharge it into the chimney. The 7-inch pipe enters the 16-inch pipe about four feet from the end furthest from the chimney, and passes through it to the chimney. A fire in the stove below will warm the foul air in the large pipe, and thus carry it away into the chimney. This fire must be made as soon as that made in the furnace or other heating apparatus, and continued as long. This church is finely heated and ventilated. [See Fig. 8.]

"Another church, which is heated by a furnace, is ventilated in the following manner: It has a chimney 16 by 36 inches inside; to secure good ventilation a hole is made through the floor near the chimney 16 by 20 inches inside; a tube is fitted into this, and reaches down into the room below, near an opening made into the chimney; an elbow connects the tube with

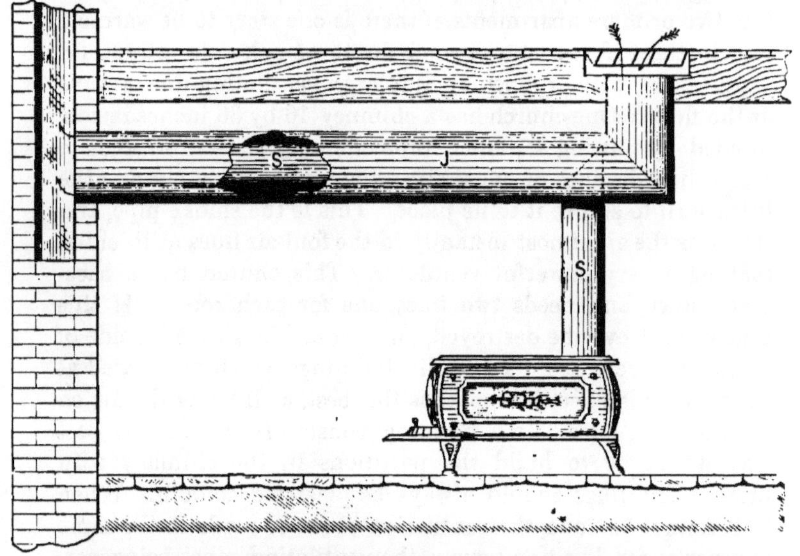

FIG. 8.—A METHOD OF VENTILATING CHURCHES. THE PIPE OF A STOVE IN THE BASEMENT IS JACKETED THROUGHOUT ITS HORIZONTAL LENGTH, THUS INDUCING A DRAFT FROM THE OPENING IN THE FLOOR ABOVE CONNECTED WITH IT. S, STOVE-PIPE. J, JACKET AROUND STOVE-PIPE.

the chimney; the foul air from the room above passes through this tube into the chimney below, and this ventilates the church, giving it pure warm air. The opening into the chimney is made below the entrance of the smoke-pipe from the furnace, so that the smoke does not enter the ventilating tube. [See Fig. 9.]

"In all these illustrations the two rules given have been observed, and may be applied in many other forms: First, conduct the outdoor air against a heated surface; second, conduct the foul air in the room from the floor into a heated flue, and good heating and ventilating will be secured."

The introduction of fresh air and removal of foul air simultaneously is accomplished in an almost perfect manner by the stove illustrated in Fig. 10. It has a large drum above the fire, surrounded by a jacket, so arranged that a constant supply of fresh air may be brought into contact with greatly-expanded surfaces, which absorb the maximum quantity of heat, and impart it

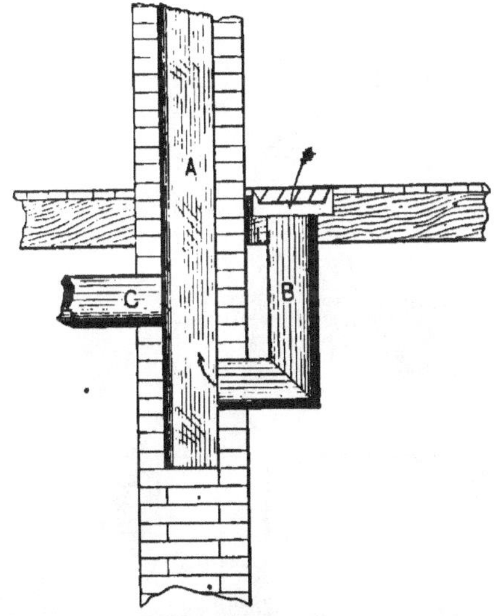

FIG. 9.—VENTILATING A CHURCH BY CONNECTING AN OPENING IN THE FLOOR WITH THE MAIN CHIMNEY FLUE, MAKING THE CONNECTION BELOW THE ENTRANCE OF THE FURNACE-PIPE. A, CHIMNEY FLUE. B, VENTILATION TUBE. C, POSITION OF FURNACE-PIPE.

rapidly to the in-flowing currents—thus preventing over-heating, and at the same time supplying the room with an abundant, genial and invigorating atmosphere. It will be observed that two distinct currents pass through the stove. One enters beneath the grate, ascends to the chamber above, passes over the diaphragm therein, and thence goes to the chimney, furnishing the draft. The other enters under the stove, and becomes heated by contact with the hot surfaces, and rises through the jacket, thus compelling a constant circulation through the latter. The fire is entirely open, so that a large supply of additional heat is radiated therefrom. The construction, evidently, is such that

FIG. 10.

there is no opportunity for leakage of the deadly carbonic acid gas; nor is there any contact of highly-heated plates with the air of the room to generate carbonic oxide.

By its use the entire atmosphere of any room may be replaced every fifteen or twenty minutes, with a supply of invigorating, refreshing out-door air, moderately warmed, and not dried, parched and devitalized; and the air supplied for breathing may be rendered as pure and refreshing as the outdoor Summer air.

And now that we are on the subject of heating, it will be in place to warn householders against too great heat and too dry heat. Too much cannot be said to impress on all householders the great value of keeping all parts of the house—halls, and best rooms, and bed-rooms—as well as the kitchen and living rooms, comfortably warm. Many a doctor's bill, many a bad cold, might be entirely prevented by attention to this matter. It should be safe for the children to go anywhere in the house without danger of catching cold. If our houses were moderately heated throughout and thoroughly ventilated, how much better it would be for all concerned, than to overheat one or two rooms in the house and religiously exclude from them God's pure air.

"Immoderate use of heat during the Winter is the cause of much illness. The effect upon the general vigor of many hours daily spent in overwarm rooms is like that of heat upon a figure in wax. It droops, loses its firmness, and, little by little, will show absolute outward change. Moreover, one of the positive results of hot air is, that it paralyzes the action of the heart. Suppose you were to put your arm in a sling, and make no use of it for three months; at the end of that time, what would be its condition? It would be weak, shrunken, almost powerless; only by a system of careful exercise of weeks in duration could its original vigor be restored.

"Now, when a person indulges in too much artificial heat, this is what happens to the skin, and, through its collapse, also happens to the system at large. A person leads a sedentary life in hot rooms. As Winter deepens, the cold grows more forbidding, the fire more seductive. Fresh air is shut out, the skin becomes less and less able to resist changes of temperature. When this person does go out of doors, no matter how much clothing he may wear, he suffers; and a cold is almost sure to result."

The danger from overheating will be greatly lessened if a large pan of water is kept continually evaporating over the stove or in the air-chamber of the furnace. It is a well-known fact that, as air becomes heated, its capacity to absorb moisture is greatly increased; and this moisture, which is naturally supplied in Summer, it is necessary for us to artificially supply to the artificial Summer we create within our houses in Winter.

A safe rule would be to wear warmer clothing in Winter, and keep the temperature of the rooms we live in not higher than 68° Fahrenheit.

In all that has been said above, the requirements of ordinary country farm houses have been kept in view, and nothing suggested which cannot be effected by a little care and forethought by the head of the household.

Those who can afford furnaces, or hot water, or steam, I refer to other and larger treatises, only let me add one word of advice to those having these apparatuses in use or contemplating their use, viz.: Be sure the furnace is (1) large enough not to overheat the air, in order to properly warm the house; (2) be sure there is a large supply of outdoor air to the air-chamber; (3) be sure there is an evaporating pan constantly filled in the air-chamber.

Those having the ventilation and heating of the

SCHOOL-HOUSE

and the church in charge, have a grave responsibility resting on their shoulders. To them is committed the care of others' lives and health. The school trustees should make it their duty to often visit the school-house and see that the supply of fresh air is adequate to the wants of the scholars. In the ordinary school-houses in Ewing, the air should be changed at least every nine minutes. This can be easily and safely accomplished by making in the ceiling at least three apertures one foot wide and two feet long, carried through the roof, and a foot or two above it, and fitted with an Emerson Ventilating Cowl, which is intended to prevent a back draught. These openings are to remove the foul air. The fresh air can then be supplied by any of the means mentioned above for houses. The surest way, however, would be by the use of the open stove with a fresh air inlet, as illustrated above. Whatever stove is used, it should be so placed that the children need not sit close to it, as the effect, particularly of sitting with the back to a hot stove, is very prejudicial to health, resulting often in congestion of the kidneys and other disorders.

It would be better to have two stoves, with a moderate fire in each, than one large stove overheated. Where there is a cellar beneath the building, it would be better to place these stoves in it, supplying fresh air to them by ducts, and then make as many as five openings in the floor, one foot by two, through

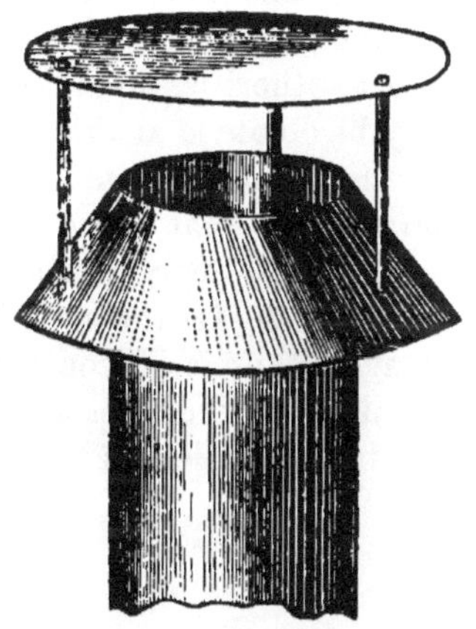

EMERSON VENTILATING COWL.

which the warmed air will rise into the room. The cellar in this case should be used for no other purpose (some other place being provided for the coal and wood), and be kept scrupulously clean; and, where wet, made dry by drainage, as shown in the note on "Drainage for Health." Whatever method is used, the school-room should be provided with thermometers, say one in each corner, which the teacher should often consult to see that the temperature is never above 68° nor below 64°.

It should be made the duty of the janitor to see that the room is thoroughly aired, by having every window and door opened immediately after the school is closed; and this airing should continue at least an hour. It should be equally the duty of the janitor to have the room warm and all the shutters open, the sun streaming in, for an hour before school assembles.

The above remarks have been written with a special view to country district school-houses, and particularly those of Ewing township, which consist of but one room with accommodations for about fifty pupils, and an average attendance of a somewhat less number.

The editor will be glad, at any time, to furnish, free of charge, to any similar schools in New Jersey, plans and suggestions for heating and ventilating, where he is given the size of the school-room (width and depth), and height of ceiling, the average number of the pupils, and the exposure. These suggestions will be submitted to the best authorities on the subject, in order that the result desired may be obtained at the least expense and in the very best way for the particular case in point.

Let me impress on teachers that the health of the children committed to their care is of vastly greater concern than the knowledge they may be able to give them. "Ordinary attention to these matters, if systematic and constant, will do much toward lessening the 'murder of the innocents,' who so frequently are the victims of their thoughtless elders."—[*Revised by Carl Pfeiffer, Arch.*

SYNOPSIS OF SUCH LAWS OF THE STATE OF NEW JERSEY AS CONCERN A RURAL COMMUNITY.

COMPILED BY A. G. RICHEY, ESQ.

Mode of Laying out Public Roads.

When ten or more persons, being freeholders, shall think a public road necessary in any part of the county, they may apply to the Court of Common Pleas of the county for the appointment of six surveyors of the highways to lay out such road.

Ten days' notice of such application must be first given.

The surveyors of the highway are to meet, at such time and place as the court shall direct, for the purpose of laying out said road.

Notice shall be given by advertisement of the time and place of such meeting.

The surveyors of the highway, when met as aforesaid, shall view the premises, and may, if they think necessary, lay out such public road; and they shall lay the same as it appears to them to be most for the public and private convenience—having a regard to the best ground for a road and the shortest distance in such a manner as to do the least injury to private property.

And they shall make a return thereof, with a map of the same, with the courses and distances, with the time when the overseers of the highway shall open the same for public use.

The said surveyors shall also make an assessment of the damages, if any, the owner of any land (other than an applicant for such road) shall sustain by laying out the same, above the advantages that will accrue to the owner, which assessment they must affix to their return, which return, with the assessments, shall be delivered to the clerk of the Court of Common Pleas of the county, who is required to record the said return, together with the map thereof, in a book to be kept for that purpose; and every road so laid out and recorded as aforesaid shall be a lawful highway from the time appointed for opening the same.

That the clerk of any Court of Common Pleas shall not record the return of the surveyors of the highway until the expiration of fifteen days after he shall have received the same, so that any person being aggrieved thereby may, within that time, enter a caveat with the said clerk against recording the said return, which shall operate as a supersedeas to further proceedings till the next court.

At the next court, the persons who have filed the caveat, may make application to the court for the appointment of six of the chosen freeholders of the county in which the road shall have been laid out.

And the court will appoint them and designate the time and place for their meeting.

Notice of such meeting to be given.

And the chosen freeholders so appointed shall proceed to view the road so laid out.

And if they or a majority of them shall believe such laying necessary and useful, they shall certify the same to the court the term next succeeding their appointment; and the court thereupon shall cause the proceedings to be recorded; and their proceedings shall be binding and conclusive in all cases; but if they shall believe such laying out to be unnecessary and injurious, they shall certify the same to the court as aforesaid, and the proceedings of the surveyors shall then be null and void.

Law to Prevent the Spread of Canada Thistle.

If any person or persons owning or having the care of any lands, enclosed or unenclosed, in this State, shall knowingly permit any Canada thistle to grow up thereon, and suffer the same to stand until its seeds get ripe, he or they shall, for every stalk or bunch thereof so suffered to grow up, forfeit and pay a fine of twenty-five cents; to be sued for and recovered, with costs, by any person, in his name, before any court of competent jurisdiction.

The Law as to the Construction of Sidewalks.

That it shall be lawful for the inhabitants of any township in this State, at their annual meeting, to provide for the construction of sidewalks on the public highway, not exceeding in width one-fifth on each side of the road of the width thereof, and also to place posts or railings by the side thereof, which sidewalks shall be constructed out of any money raised for the repairs of highways; and the amount so to be expended, and the road or place where the sidewalks shall be made, shall be determined by such meeting or by the township committee; provided, that this provision shall not apply to any public highway, which hath been or which shall be hereafter laid out, of a less width than three rods, except in such place or places where it shall pass through a city, town, or village.

And it shall be lawful for any person owning or occupying lands adjoining a public road or highway in any township, city, or ward, to construct sidewalks on said highway in the manner hereinbefore provided, contiguous and along the line of said land.

That when a sidewalk shall have been constructed as aforesaid, every person who shall ride or drive a horse or team thereon, except for the purpose of crossing the same, when necessary so to do, shall forfeit and pay the sum of five dollars to the use of the township, to be sued for and recovered by any person who shall sue for the same.

SUPPLEMENT TO THE FOREGOING ACT.

That the provisions of the act to which this is a supplement, shall not authorize the construction of sidewalks of a greater width than five feet on each side of any public road or highway in this State, which hath been or which shall hereafter be laid out of a less width than three rods, except in such place or places where they pass through the cities, towns, or villages of this State.

As to Working and Maintaining Public Roads.

The township committee who shall be hereafter chosen agreeably to law, in the respective townships of this State, or a majority of such committee, are hereby authorized and directed to assign and appoint, in writing, to the overseers of the highways, respectively, their several limits and divisions of the highways within such township, for opening, clearing out, working, amendment and repair, and the said overseers are hereby commanded to observe and conform themselves to such assignment.

That it shall be the duty of the said overseers to hire laborers, and also horses, oxen, wagons, ploughs, carts and other implements to open, clear out, make, work, amend, repair and keep in good order the highways within their respective limits and divisions, to make causeways, and to erect such bridges as can be built by common laborers, and to procure whatever materials they shall deem necessary to effect the purposes specified in this section.

That the moneys necessary for defraying the costs, charges and expenses of opening, clearing out, making, working, amending, repairing and keeping in good order the highways, and procuring materials for the same, and also the compensation allowed for the services of the overseers thereof, shall be granted, assessed, collected and raised in the manner prescribed by the act entitled "An act incorporating the inhabitants of townships, designating their powers and regulating their meetings"; and it is hereby enjoined upon the said townships, that they be careful to have money in hand ready to advance sufficient for the objects and purposes specified in this act.

Law as to Cutting Down Trees Along Highways.

That no overseer of the highways or other person, except the owner or owners thereof, shall cut down, willfully injure, or destroy any fruit, shade or ornamental tree which may have been or which shall be planted or set out by the owner or possessor of lands adjoining any highway in this State, and which shall not extend more than seven feet out from the line of the road towards the center of the same, unless the township committee of the township in which such road is situate, or a majority of such committee, shall first order the cutting down or destroying of the same.

That if any overseer of the highway or other person shall offend against the provisions of the preceding section, he, she or they so offending shall forfeit and pay the sum of fifty dollars for each and every such offence, to be recovered in an action of debt, with costs of suit, in any court having cognizance thereof, by any person who may prosecute for the same, within six months after such offence shall have been committed, provided that this act shall not prevent any overseer from clearing out any highways to their full width where they pass through any wood or forest.

Law Against Girdling Trees Along Highways.

That no tree shall be girdled or killed on the highways, under the penalty of two dollars, to be recovered by action of debt, with costs, by the overseer of the highways, in any court of record having cognizance of that sum, and applied to the working and repair of the highways; and if any such tree shall be girdled or killed in the manner aforesaid, it shall be the duty of the said overseer forthwith to cut down such tree so girdled or killed.

That if any person shall girdle or kill any tree standing within two rods of such highway, the owner or possessor of the land where the same stands shall, within two years after such girdling or killing, cut down the said tree; or, on failure thereof, shall forfeit and pay two dollars, to be recovered and applied in the manner above set forth.

The Law as to Wheel Carriages.

That all wagons and other wheel carriages of any kind or description whatever, drawn by one or more horse or horses, oxen, or other cattle, made and constructed, and all axle-trees made or repaired from and after the first day of October, A.D. 1874, traveling or passing on or through the roads or highways within this State, belonging to persons resident therein, shall run or track on the ground, from center to center of the felloes, not less than four feet and ten inches, under the penalty of five dollars, to be recovered from the owner or owners, proprietor or proprietors of such wagon or other wheel carriage, for each and every offence, before any one justice of the peace of this State, where the fact shall be committed, upon the oath or affirmation of one or more witness or witnesses. Which said fine, when recovered, shall be paid, one moiety thereof to the overseers of the highways for the township, division, or precinct where the fact was committed, to be applied toward the repair of the highways within the same; and the other moiety to be paid to the person or persons prosecuting the same to effect; and the said overseers are hereby made accountable for all moneys they may receive in virtue of this act, in the same manner and form as they are for other fines and forfeitures; provided, always, that the above fines shall not be set or levied more than once upon one journey, and that every information relative to any breach of this act be made within twenty days after the offence is committed.

Respecting Railroads and Canals.

Every incorporated company that hath been or hereafter may be authorized to construct any railroad in this State, shall cause to be placed on some part of every locomotive engine used by any such company, a bell of a weight of not less than thirty pounds, or steam whistle which can be heard distinctly at a distance of at least three hundred yards from the place where any such railroad crosses a turnpike road or highway upon the same level with the said railroad, and such bell shall be kept ringing, or such whistle shall continue to be blown, until the engine has crossed such turnpike or highway, or has stopped.

And any railroad company which shall construct any railroad by virtue of powers granted in their charter by this State, may, in crossing any public highway, for the purpose of making such highway cross over or under such railroad at an easy and suitable grade, alter the location of such highway at their own expense, so far as shall be necessary to make such highway pass over or under said railroad at such grade, and such alteration shall be valid and of the same effect as if made by surveyors of the highway according to law. And all alterations heretofore made in any public highway in this State, by any such railroad company, for the purpose and in the manner aforesaid, are hereby confirmed and made valid as if the same had been made by the surveyors of the highway according to law.

If any person shall be injured by a locomotive engine, car or cars while walking, standing or playing on any railroad in this State, or by jumping on or off a car while in motion, such person shall be deemed to have contributed to the injury sustained, and shall not recover any damages therefor from the company owning or operating the said railroad; provided, however, that this section shall not apply to any person or persons crossing a railroad at any lawful public or private crossing.

Every railroad company shall cause a board with this inscription, "Look out for the locomotive," to be erected and maintained wherever the road of such company may be crossed by any turnpike road or public highway, so as to be easily seen by travelers.

If any such company shall refuse or neglect to comply with the foregoing provisions, they shall forfeit for every such refusal or neglect, the sum of one hundred dollars, to be sued for by the clerk of any township in which such refusal or neglect shall occur, for the use of said township, and to be recovered, with costs, in action of debt in any court having cognizance thereof; provided, that all complaints of any refusal or neglect to comply with said provisions shall have been made within ten days thereafter; and, provided further, that nothing herein contained shall be construed to take away from any individual or individuals any right he, she or they may have to recover damages for any injury which may be incurred by any refusal or neglect to comply with the requirements of this act.

If any person shall willfully obliterate, destroy or injure any such board so as aforesaid erected, he, she or they so offending shall forfeit for every such offence the sum of twenty dollars, to be recovered, with costs, by any such railroad company, in an action of debt before any court having cognizance thereof, for the use of said company.

The Law as to the Width of Public Roads.

That every public road or highway which shall be hereafter laid out shall not be more than four rods wide, unless a greater width shall be specified in the notices and applications for the same; nor shall any such road be less than two rods wide, unless the same be laid out in a village, borough or city, and where, by reason of buildings or other permanent erections, such road cannot be, conveniently, laid out of such width.

That every private road which shall be hereafter laid out shall not be more than thirty feet in width, but may be less, at the discretion of the surveyors.

The Law to Prevent the Defacement of Natural Scenery.

That without the previous consent of the owner, all persons are hereafter prohibited from advertising their wares or occupation, by printed notices of the same, on fences or other private property, or upon cliffs or rocks or other natural objects.

And all persons violating the provisions of the above paragraph shall be punished by a fine of ten dollars for each offence, to be recovered before a justice of the peace; the action to be brought in debt, in the corporate name of the township, borough or city in which such offence shall be committed; one-half of which said fine shall be for the use of the informer or prosecutor of such action, the other half to the overseer of the poor of the township, borough or city in which such offence shall have been committed.

Malicious Mischief.

Whosoever shall unlawfully and maliciously pull, or throw down, or in anywise destroy any bridge, whether over any stream of water or otherwise, under which bridge any highway, railway or canal shall pass, or do any injury with intent, and so as thereby to render such bridge, viaduct, or the highway, railway or canal passing over or under the same, or any part thereof, dangerous or impassable, shall be guilty of a misdemeanor, and shall be liable to imprisonment at hard labor, not over one year, or fine, not over two hundred dollars, or both.

As to Certain Crimes.

Whoever shall unlawfully and maliciously destroy or damage any statue, bust or vase, or any other article or thing kept for the purpose of art, science or literature, or as an object of curiosity in any museum, gallery, cabinet, library or other repository, which museum, gallery, cabinet, library or other repository is open for the admission of the public, or of any considerable number of persons, to view the same, either by permission of the proprietor thereof, or by the payment of money before entering the same; or any picture, statue, monument, or other memorial of the dead, or other ornament in any church or other place of divine worship, or in any building, or in any church-yard, burial ground, or public garden or ground, or any ornament, railing or fence surrounding such statue or monument, shall be guilty of a misdemeanor, and, being convicted thereof, shall be liable to be imprisoned for any term not exceeding six months, or fined two hundred dollars.

Whosoever shall steal or cut, break, root up, or otherwise destroy or damage, with intent to steal, the whole or any part of any tree, sapling or shrub, or any underwood or plant, root, fruit or vegetable production, wheresoever the same may be growing, or shall steal, or shall cut, break or throw down, with intent to steal, any fence or any wooden post, pale, wire or rail set up or used as a fence, or any stile or gate, or any part thereof, respectively, he shall be guilty of a misdemeanor, and, on conviction thereof, shall be liable to be punished as in case of larceny.

As to Disorderly Persons.

Any person who shall enter the buildings or go upon the lands belonging to any public school district of this State, or used and occupied for school purposes, by any public school in this State, and shall break, injure or deface such building, or any part thereof, or the fences or out-houses belonging to or connected with such building or lands, or shall disturb the exercises of such public school, or molest or give annoyance to the children attending such school, or any teacher therein, shall be deemed and adjudged to be a disorderly person, and may be apprehended in the manner hereinafter described in this act, and taken before any justice of the peace of the county where such person may be apprehended. And it shall be the duty of the said justice to commit such disorderly person, when convicted before him by the confession of the offender or by the oath or affirmation of one or more witnesses, to the county jail of such county, there to be kept at hard labor for any term not exceeding thirty days.

An Act to Define and Suppress Tramps.

That the following described persons are hereby declared to be tramps: All persons who shall come from any place without this State, or from any city, county, township, borough or place in this State, and have no legal settlement in the places in which they are found, and live idly and without employment, and refuse to work for the usual and common wages given to other persons for like work in the place where they then are, or shall be found going about from door to door, or placing themselves in the streets, highways or roads to beg or gather alms, and can give no reasonable account of themselves or their business in such places.

That if any person shall be found offending in any county, city, township, borough or district in this State, against this act, it shall and may be lawful for any constable or police officer of such place, and he is hereby enjoined and required, on notice thereof to him given by any of the inhabitants thereof, or without such notice, on his own view, to apprehend and convey, or cause to be conveyed, such person to a justice of the peace or other magistrate of such place, who shall examine such person, and shall commit him or her, being thereof legally convicted before him, on his own view, or by the confession of such offenders, or by the oath or affirmation of one or more credible witnesses, to labor upon any county farm or upon the streets, roads and highways of any city, township or borough, or in any house of correction, poor-house, work-house or common jail, for a term not exceeding six months, and shall forthwith commit him or her to the custody of the steward, keeper or superintendent of such county farm, house of correction, poor-house, work-house or common jail, or to the supervisors or overseers of the highways, street commissioners, or other officer or officers having in charge the repairs of any street, road or highway, or overseers of the poor of the respective township, borough, county or city wherein such person shall be found, as in their judgment shall be deemed most expedient.

An Act to Prevent Trespassing with Guns.

If any person or persons shall carry any gun on any land not his own, and for which the owner pays taxes, or is in his lawful possession, unless he hath license or permission in writing from the owner or owners or legal possessor, every such person so offending, and convicted thereof, either upon the view of any justice of the peace within this State, or by the oath or affirmation of one or more witnesses, before any justice of the peace within this State, or by the oath or affirmation of one or more witnesses, before any justice of the peace of either of the counties, cities or towns corporate, of this State, in which the offender may be taken or reside, he shall, for every such offence, forfeit and pay to the owner of the soil, or his tenant in possession, the sum of five dollars, with costs of suit; which forfeiture may and shall be sued for and recovered by the owner of the soil or tenant in possession, before any justice of the peace in this State, for the use of such owner or tenant in possession.

Law to Prevent the Adulteration of Milk.

If any person shall knowingly sell any impure or unwholesome milk, he shall be deemed guilty of a misdemeanor, and on conviction thereof, he shall be punished by a fine of not less than fifty dollars for each and every offence.

And if any person shall adulterate milk with a view of offering the same for sale, he shall be deemed guilty of a misdemeanor, and on conviction thereof shall be punished by a fine of not less than fifty dollars for each and every offence.

The addition of water to milk is hereby declared to be an adulteration thereof.

Law for the Prevention of Cruelty to Animals.

That any person who shall overdrive, overload, overwork, cruelly beat or otherwise abuse any living animal, and any person having the charge of any living animal, who inflicts unnecessary cruelty upon the same, or fails to provide the same with proper food, drink or shelter, or protection from the weather, shall be deemed guilty of a misdemeanor, and for every such offence, shall, on conviction thereof, be punished, by fine not exceeding two hundred dollars, or by imprisonment in the county jail not exceeding six months, or both, in the discretion of the court.

And any person who shall keep or use any place for the purpose of fighting or baiting any bull, bear, dog, cock, or other living animal or creature, and every person who shall be present and witness, encourage, aid or assist therein, shall be deemed guilty of a misdemeanor, and for every such offence, shall, on conviction thereof, be punished by fine not exceeding one thousand dollars, or by imprisonment at hard labor not exceeding two years, or both, at the discretion of the court.

And any person who shall use any dog or dogs for the purpose of drawing any cart or other vehicle for business or other purposes, shall forfeit and pay a fine of one dollar for the first offence and ten dollars for each subsequent offence—such offender, together with the dog, cart or other vehicle shall be taken before a justice of the peace or police magistrate, who, upon being satisfied, shall impose said fine, which said fine, as soon as imposed, shall have the force and effect of a judgment, and execution may be immediately issued thereon, and the articles so seized levied upon and sold to pay and satisfy the said fine, together with the costs.

That if a maimed, sick, infirm or disabled animal shall be abandoned to die, by any person, in any public place, such person shall be deemed guilty of a misdemeanor, and on conviction thereof shall be punished as provided for in the beginning of this article. That any person who shall overdrive, overwork, torture, deprive of necessary sustenance, or cruelly beat or otherwise abuse or kill, any living animal or creature, and every person who shall be present, and witness, encourage or assist therein, shall forfeit and pay such sum, not exceeding one hundred dollars, as the court shall determine, to be sued for and recovered in an action of debt, with costs of suit, by any person, in the name of "The New Jersey Society for the Prevention of Cruelty to Animals."

An Act for the Preservation of Sheep.

When any person shall sustain damage or injury by reason of his or her sheep or lambs being killed or wounded by a dog or dogs, wolf or wolves, it shall be lawful for such person to take two respectable freeholders of the township wherein such damage was done, who are in nowise akin to the party so calling them, to view the sheep or lambs so killed or wounded, and if it shall appear to their satisfaction that the said sheep or lambs were killed or wounded by a dog or dogs, wolf or wolves, then the said freeholders shall make a return or certificate thereof in writing, stating the amount of damages such person may have sustained, which shall in no case exceed five dollars for one sheep or lamb so killed or wounded, which said certificate shall entitle the person so injured to the sum stated therein as the damage sustained, to be paid by the township committee, in conformity to the provisions made therefor in the fifth section of this act. And in case the damage so certified shall appear to the town committee to be excessive, it shall and may be lawful for said committee to require the facts stated and the claim exhibited, to be investigated before them on oath or affirmation, and shall award payment accordingly. Provided always, that nothing herein contained shall extend to cases wherein a recovery of damages can be obtained of the owner or owners of such dog or dogs as shall have committed the injury.

Protection Against Mad Dogs.

The mayor of any incorporated town in this State, by the advice and consent of the common council of the town, and the township clerk of any township in this State, by the advice of the township committee, are authorized, whenever, in their opinion, the public safety may require, to issue his proclamation authorizing the destruction of all dogs, male and female, found running at large within the limits of the town, except such as shall be properly muzzled with a wire muzzle about the nose, securely fastened, after one day's public notice by written or printed hand-bills; provided, that nothing in said proclamation shall apply to a dog or dogs of a non-resident passing through the town accompanied by the owner or owners of such dog or dogs.

An Act to Prevent Spread of Contagious Diseases Amongst Cattle.

The town committee of each township of this State, upon notice of the existence of any disease among cattle in their township, are authorized personally to examine the cases, and if the symptoms which characterize contagious diseases are exhibited, they shall cause such sick animals to be immediately removed and kept separate from all other cattle; and the remaining cattle of said owner shall be kept isolated from the sick ones, and both they and the sick animals shall be kept distant at least four hundred feet from the public road, and the same distance from the premises of all neighbors.

The town committee are also authorized to prohibit the importation of cattle from other places into or through their respective township; and if any one shall import or drive any cattle into or through any township after the same shall have been publicly prohibited by the town committee, he shall pay a fine of one hundred dollars for every bull, ox, steer, cow, heifer or calf so driven into a township. Any person who shall dispose of any cattle or stock, knowing it to be subject to any contagious disease, shall pay a fine of one hundred dollars for any such animal sold within the township.

The persons qualified to vote at town meetings are authorized at their annual meetings to make such provision and allow such rewards for the destruction of wolves, wild-cats, foxes, crows, black-birds, and other noxious wild animals and birds, as they so assembled shall deem necessary or proper.

Destruction of Insectiverous, Small and Harmless Birds.

That it shall not be lawful for any person to wantonly shoot, entrap for the purpose of killing, or in any other manner destroy any upland birds whose principal food is insects, comprised in the families of swallows, fly-catchers, finches, larks, wood-peckers and other species and varieties of land birds of every description regarded as harmless in their habits, and whose flesh is unfit for food, excepting the eagle, raven, crow, all hawks and owls which prey upon other birds, and that it shall not be lawful for any person to take or destroy the eggs or young of any of the species of birds which are intended to be protected by this act.

And if complaint is made, under oath, before any justice of the peace of this State, of any violation of the foregoing provisions, it shall be the duty of such justice to forthwith issue, under his hand and seal, a warrant against the person or persons so offending, and the proceedings before the justice shall be regulated according to the provisions of the act entitled "An act constituting courts for the trial of small causes."

And every person offending against the provisions of this act, shall, on conviction, be fined in any sum not less than ten or more than twenty dollars, with costs of suit, in the discretion of the court before whom such conviction shall be had.

As the school law is published in full in pamphlet form, it has not been thought worth while to make any extracts therefrom; but the editor would call attention to that provision of the law which authorizes the State Superintendent to pay to any school, which shall raise twenty dollars by subscription for a library or for philosophical apparatus, a like sum to be used for the same purpose. Furthermore, so long, after the first year, as a school raises ten dollars a year for the above purpose, the State will add a like sum.

The following clipping, from the "Princeton Press" of September 11th, 1880, is respectfully

DEDICATED TO THE LADIES.

"THE WEST EWING IMPROVEMENT ASSOCIATION.

"The second annual meeting of this Association was held in the Ewing Church, Thursday afternoon. There was a large attendance, evincing interest in the Association's work. But that which showed the deepest interest in the meeting was the evident labor bestowed on the decoration of the edifice. The audience-room has a very pleasing appearance of itself, and, as decorated, it was perfectly beautiful. Crossed sheaves of 'golden grain' placed against the closed inside blinds, were in the center of each window, crowned with the national colors; large vases on each window-sill were filled with plants and flowers; a spray of evergreen relieved each side bracket; the book-rack in each pew was banked with green, interspersed with bouquets and cut flowers, while a wreath of the same fragrance and beauty was carried along the top of the dividing line between the rows of pews. The platform was graced with a variety of rare plants, and the initials of the Association, in evergreen, formed a background for the whole. Altogether it has not been our pleasure to have ever seen more tasteful decorations.

"Hon. A. B. Green, President, presided. Rev. Dr. Lowrie, pastor of the church, and a member of the society, offered prayer. Musical selections from Auber, Liszt, Meyerbeer, and Mendelssohn were played on the piano and organ, of course in a masterly way, by Prof. Allmuth and Mr. Van Kuren."

CONSTITUTION

OF THE

WEST EWING IMPROVEMENT ASSOCIATION.

We, the residents of the township of Ewing, county of Mercer and State of New Jersey, in order to form an Association to improve and ornament the public roads and grounds, do ordain and establish this Constitution for said Association.

ARTICLE I.

This Association shall be called "THE WEST EWING IMPROVEMENT ASSOCIATION."

ARTICLE II.

The object of this Association shall be to improve and ornament the public roads and grounds of the township, by planting and cultivating trees, establishing and maintaining walks, grading and draining the roadways, providing public drinking troughs, breaking out paths through the snow, lighting canal bridges, and generally doing whatever may tend to the improvement of the township as a place of residence.

ARTICLE III.

The officers of this Association shall be a President, two Vice-Presidents, a Secretary and a Treasurer, who shall constitute the Executive Committee.

The officers shall be elected at the annual meeting, (except for the first election, which shall take place October 8th, 1878,) and shall hold their offices until their successors have been elected.

ARTICLE IV.

It shall be the duty of the President, and, in his absence, of the senior Vice-President, to preside at all meetings of the

Association, and to carry out all orders of the Executive Committee.

ARTICLE V.

It shall be the duty of the Secretary to keep a correct and careful record of all proceedings of the Association and of the Executive Committee, in a book suitable for their preservation; to give notice of all meetings of the Association and of the Executive Committee; to make all publications, and to give all public and private notices ordered by the Executive Committee, and to attend to all correspondence of the Association.

ARTICLE VI.

It shall be the duty of the Treasurer to keep the funds of the Association, and to make such disbursements as may be ordered by the Executive Committee.

ARTICLE VII.

It shall be the duty of the Executive Committee to employ all laborers, make all contracts, expend all moneys, and generally to direct and superintend all improvements which, in their discretion, and with the means at their command, will best serve the public interest.

The Executive Committee shall hold a meeting at least once a month, and as much oftener as they may deem expedient.

The Executive Committee shall have power to institute premiums to be awarded for planting and protecting ornamental trees, and for doing such other acts as may seem to them worthy of such encouragement. They shall also encourage frequent public meetings of the Association, and of citizens generally, both with a view to maintain an interest in their work, and for the general encouragement of meeting together for discussion and amusement.

It shall be the duty of the Executive Committee to obtain the preparation of papers on topics directly bearing on the work of the Association, which shall be read at the social meetings.

ARTICLE VIII.

Auxiliary to the Executive Committee there shall be subcommittees of an advisory nature, whose duty it shall be to promote the objects of the Association in their district, by interesting all members of the community in the work, and suggesting improvements most needed in their immediate neighborhoods.

These committees shall be especially charged with preserving and carefully providing for the safety of trees planted, and other improvements effected in their districts. They shall be composed of two ladies and one gentleman, and shall offer their suggestions at the social meetings.

These committees shall be appointed by the President of the Association.

ARTICLE IX.

Three members of the Executive Committee, present at any meeting, shall constitute a quorum for transacting business, and a vote of the majority of those present shall be binding on the Association.

ARTICLE X.

No debt shall be contracted by the Executive Committee beyond the amount of available funds within their control to pay it; and no member of the Association shall be liable for any debt of the Association beyond the amount of his or her subscription.

ARTICLE XI.

Every person over fourteen years of age, who shall plant a tree under the direction of the Executive Committee, and obligate himself or herself to protect it for three years, or who shall pay the sum of one dollar annually, shall be a member of this Association, and every child under fourteen years of age, who shall pay the sum of twenty-five cents annually, shall be a member of this Association.

ARTICLE XII.

The payment of ten dollars annually for three years, or twenty-five dollars in one sum, shall constitute a person a member of this Association for life.

ARTICLE XIII.

The autograph signatures of all members of the Association shall be preserved in a book suitable for that purpose.

ARTICLE XIV.

An annual meeting of the Association shall be held at such a place as the Executive Committee may direct, on the fourth Wednesday of August, at two o'clock P.M. Notice of such meeting shall be posted at the five most public places in the district, at least seven days prior to the time of holding said meeting, and a written notice shall be sent to all non-resident members. Other meetings of the Association may be called by the Executive Committee, on due notice being given.

ARTICLE XV.

At the annual meeting, the Executive Committee shall report the amount of money received during the year, and the source from which it has been received; the amount of money expended during the year, and the objects for which it has been expended; the number of trees planted at the cost of the Association; the number planted by individuals, with the location, the kind of tree and the name of the planter, and generally all of the acts of the committee. This report shall be entered on the record of the Association.

ARTICLE XVI.

Any person who shall plant a tree under the direction of the Executive Committee, and shall protect it for five years, shall be entitled to have such tree known forever by his or her name.

ARTICLE XVII.

This Constitution may be amended by the Executive Committee, with the approval of the majority of the members present, at any annual meeting of the Association, or at any special meeting, the notice of which shall have been accompanied by a copy of the proposed amendment, with the statement that the amendment is to be voted on at such meeting.

BY-LAWS.

I. The Executive Committee shall grant a certificate of merit, of an artistic design, to such of the school children as shall be certified by their teachers to have shown special zeal in keeping the surroundings of the school-houses neat and clean, or in beautifying them in any way. These certificates to be presented by the President—the committee, or some of them, being present—on the first Wednesday in June, at the morning session for Scudder's Falls, and afternoon session for Birmingham and Brookville.

II. RULES FOR TREE PLANTING.

1. Trees shall be planted on the road side of the line, and at a distance of four feet therefrom, except in the case of roads two rods wide and under, when the permission of the property-holder shall be obtained, to set them one foot from the line, in the field.

2. The trees shall be set apart a distance of 150 feet, the opposite rows alternating.

3. The following trees are recommended as best for road planting, viz.: Sugar Maple, Norway Maple, Elm, White Ash, Linden, Horse Chestnut, Water Birch, Mountain Ash, and occasionally a fruit tree.

III. The members of this Association shall, as a body and as individuals, use their influence to prevent the erection of advertising placards of any description, and to this end mutually agree to remove or cause to be removed, within ten days from June 1st, 1879, any such signs on the property of any of them, whether painted on barns, fences or stones, or nailed or pasted on trees or fences, or otherwise constructed, except legal notices and the usual advertisements of church festivals, which latter shall be allowed to stand for ten days before the date of the festival.

IV. Hereafter any person, upon compliance with Article XI of the Constitution, may be elected a member of this Association, on the nomination of any member whose dues are paid, and a vote of two-thirds of the members whose dues are paid.

V. No charge shall be made for the patent road-scraper for private use, by members of the Association. To all others, and for work on the public roads, the charge shall be five dollars per day, the Association furnishing a man to work the machine (whom the Executive Committee shall pay a sum not to exceed one dollar and a quarter), but no team. In all cases the consent of the Executive Committee must first be obtained.

LIST OF BOOKS

Which will be found valuable to those interested in Rural and Sanitary Improvement Associations.

Air and Its Relations to Life, by W. N. Hartley. $1.50.

A Pictorial Guide to Domestic Sanitary Defects, by T. Pridgin Teale, M.A., Surgeon to the General Infirmary at Leeds. With 55 lithographs. 8vo. $4.

A Treatise on Ventilation, by Lewis W. Leeds. $2.50.

Drainage for Profit and Draining for Health, by George E. Waring, Jr. $1.50.

Frankland's Water Analysis for Sanitary Purposes. $1.

Hassell's Food and Its Adulterations.

Health and Comfort in House Building, by J. Drysdale, M.D., and J. W. Hayward, M.D. Second Edition. $3.

Healthy Houses, by Wm. Eassie. $1.

Healthy Houses, by Fleming Jenkin, F.R.S., adapted to American Conditions by George E. Waring, Jr. Harpers' Half-Hour Series. 25 cents.

Heat, as applied to the Useful Arts, for the Use of Engineers, Architects, etc., by Thomas Box. $5.

House Drainage and Water Service, by James C. Bayles. $3.

Lecture on Water Supply, Sewage and Sewage Utilization, by W. H. Corfield, M.A. 50 cents.

Parkes' Hygiene, edited by De Chaumont. $6.

Sanitary Engineering, by Baldwin Latham.

Sanitary Engineering, by J. Bailey Denton.

Sanitary Work in Towns and Villages, by Charles Slagg.

The House and Its Surroundings. 40 cents.

The Sanitary Drainage of Houses and Towns, by George E. Waring, Jr. $2.

Villages and Village Life, by Rev. N. H. Eggleston. $1.75.

Village Improvements and Farm Villages, by Col. George E. Waring, Jr. 75 cents.

Wanklyn and Chapman's Water Analysis. $2.50.

Wilson's Hand-Book of Hygiene. $3.

Any of the above books may be obtained at the office of The Sanitary Engineer, 140 William Street, New York. P. O. Box 3037.

INDEX.

www.ingramcontent.com/pod-product-compliance
Lightning Source LLC
Chambersburg PA
CBHW030620270326
41927CB00007B/1248

* 9 7 8 3 3 3 7 0 0 2 7 6 3 *